FINAL
VERDICT

FINAL VERDICT

*What Really Happened
in the Rosenberg Case*

By WALTER SCHNEIR

With Preface and Afterword by
MIRIAM SCHNEIR

MELVILLEHOUSE
BROOKLYN, NEW YORK

Melville House Publishing and Miriam Schneir
acknowledge with thanks a grant provided by the
National Committee to Reopen the Rosenberg Case.

First printing: September 2010
Book design by Kelly Blair
Library of Congress Cataloging-in-Publication Data

Schneir, Walter.
 Final verdict / by Walter Schneir ; with preface and afterword by Miriam Schneir.
 — 1st U.S. ed.
    p. cm.
 Includes index.
 ISBN 978-1-935554-16-5
 1. Rosenberg, Julius, 1918-1953. 2. Rosenberg, Ethel, 1915-1953. 3. Sobell, Morton.
 4. Trials (Espionage)—New York (State)—New York. I. Schneir, Miriam. II. Title.
 HX84.R6S27 2010
 364.1'31—dc22
                                    2010014535

CONTENTS

SOVIET ATOMIC ESPIONAGE, 1940s	CONTEXT
Aug. 1941. Klaus Fuchs recruited by Soviets in England	1941. Nazi Germany begins to implement the Final Solution to the "Jewish problem"
Late 1941. Julius Rosenberg recruited by Soviet agent in NY	June 22, 1941. Hitler invades USSR
	Dec. 7, 1941. Japan bombs Pearl Harbor; U.S. enters WWII
	Dec. 2, 1942. Enrico Fermi creates the world's first controlled nuclear chain reaction, Chicago
	Feb. 2, 1943. Germans surrender at Stalingrad
1943–Feb. 1945. Klaus Fuchs provides information to Harry Gold in NY and Cambridge, MA.	1944. NKVD chief Lavrenty Beria and physicist Igor Kurchatov are put in charge of project to build a Soviet A-bomb
Feb. 1944–Feb. 1945. Julius passes information from "Persian" to Soviets in NY	
Sept. 1944. Ruth Greenglass recruited by	

Julius in NY

Nov. 1944. David Greenglass recruited by Ruth in Albuquerque, NM

Nov. 1944, Mar. 1945, and Apr. or May 1945. Theodore Hall provides data to Soviets in NY and NM

Jan. 1945. David and Ruth give information on Los Alamos to Julius in NY

Jan. 1945. David meets a Russian in a car in NY

Feb. 1945. Julius fired from his job with U.S. Signal Corps; Soviets reassign his contacts

Mar.–May 1945. "Persian" gives information to KGB agent Anatoli Yakovlev in NY

June 2, 1945. Fuchs gives data to Gold in Santa Fe

June 3, 1945. David and Ruth give sketches and information to Gold in Albuquerque

Apr. 12, 1945. President Franklin D. Roosevelt dies and Harry S Truman becomes president

May 8, 1945. Germans surrender to Allies

July 16, 1945. First atomic bomb exploded, Alamogordo, NM

Aug. 6, 1945. U.S. drops A-bomb on Hiroshima

Sept. 2, 1945. Japan signs surrender; WWII ends

Aug. 18, 1945. Hall gives information on A-bomb to Lona Cohen in Albuquerque

Sept. 19, 1945. Fuchs gives information on A-bomb to Gold in Santa Fe

Sept. 21, 1945. David meets with Yakovlev in NY; Yakovlev reports to Moscow that David has given Soviets A-bomb information and a cartridge for a detonator but does not mention place or date of delivery

Dec. 21, 1945. Yakovlev schedules a meeting between Ruth and Lona Cohen

Sept. 5, 1945. Soviet code clerk Igor Gouzenko defects, Ottawa, Canada

Fall 1945. Moscow orders suspension of intelligence activities in U.S.

Nov. 1945. Spy courier Elizabeth Bentley defects, NY

ARRESTS & TRIALS	CONTEXT
	1947. Attorney General's list of subversive organizations compiled
	1947. House Un-American Activities Committee begins investigation of Communists in Hollywood
	Apr. 1949. Smith Act trial of top U.S. Communist Party leaders opens in NY
Feb. 2, 1950. Klaus Fuchs arrested in London and confesses	Aug. 29, 1949. First atomic explosion in USSR
May 23, 1950. Harry Gold arrested in Philadelphia and confesses	Construction of fallout shelters begins in U.S.
June 16,1950. David Greenglass arrested in NY and confesses	1950. Congress passes Internal Security Act
July 17, 1950. Julius Rosenberg arrested in NY	Jan. 1950. Alger Hiss convicted
Aug. 11, 1950. Ethel Rosenberg arrested in NY	Feb. 1950. Sen. Joseph McCarthy accuses U.S. State Dept. of harboring Communists
Aug. 16-18, 1950. Morton Sobell kidnapped from Mexico, driven to border, and arrested	June 25, 1950. Korean War begins

Mar. 1, 1950. Klaus Fuchs tried and found guilty, sentenced to 14 years

Dec. 7, 1950. Harry Gold sentencing hearing, sentenced to 30 years

1951. National Committee to Secure Justice in the Rosenberg Case formed

Mar. 6-28, 1951. Trial of Rosenbergs, Sobell, and David Greenglass before Judge Irving R. Kaufman:

- Julius Rosenberg found guilty, sentenced to death
- Ethel Rosenberg found guilty, sentenced to death
- Morton Sobell found guilty, sentenced to 30 years
- David Greenglass sentenced to 15 years

Oct. 13, 1952. Supreme Court refuses to review Rosenberg case

June 19, 1953. Supreme Court reverses last-minute stay of execution granted by Justice

1952. Film "I Was a Communist for the FBI" opens, nominated for Academy Award

1952. First U.S. hydrogen bomb exploded

1952. Execution of Rudolf Slansky and ten other defendants in Czech show trial

Nov. 1952. Eisenhower elected president

Mar. 5, 1953. Death of Joseph Stalin

July 17, 1953. Korean ceasefire signed

Dec. 1953. Beria executed in USSR

1954. Roy Cohn interferes in Army affairs; Army-McCarthy hearings; Senate censures McCarthy

William O. Douglas by
6-3 vote

June 19, 1953. Rosenbergs
executed before sundown

1961. Lona and Morris
Cohen convicted of
postwar spying in
England, sentenced to
20 years

1954. Atomic Energy
Commission revokes
J. Robert Oppenheimer's
security clearance

Feb. 1956. Nikita
Khrushchev speech
denouncing Stalin and
the "cult of personality"

1960. David Greenglass
paroled

Nov. 1960. John F.
Kennedy elected
President
1963. U.S. and USSR
sign treaty ending
nuclear weapons tests in
atmosphere
Nov. 1963. Kennedy
assassinated
Nov. 1963. Lyndon
Johnson becomes
president
1964-1975. Vietnam
conflict
Antiwar, civil rights, and
feminist movements arise
1968. Assassinations of
Robert Kennedy and
Martin Luther King
1968. Police riot against
protesters at Republican
National Convention,
Chicago
Nov. 1968. Richard Nixon
elected President
July and Aug., 1974.
Watergate break-in leads
to Nixon impeachment
and resignation

1965. *Invitation to an Inquest*
by Walter and Miriam
Schneir published
1966. Morton Sobell
appeal filed
1966. Harry Gold paroled
1969. Morton Sobell
paroled
1973. *The Implosion
Conspiracy* by attorney
Louis Nizer published
1974. Congress amends
Freedom of Information
Act
1975. Michael and
Robert (Rosenberg)
Meeropol seek release of
government files on case
1975. Morton Sobell

publishes *On Doing Time*

1975. Meeropols publish *We Are Your Sons: The Legacy of Ethel and Julius Rosenberg*

1983. New edition of *Invitation to an Inquest*

1983. *The Rosenberg File* by Ronald Radosh and Joyce Milton declares Julius guilty, Ethel complicit

Oct. 1992. Anatoli Yatskov identified as KGB agent "Yakovlev"

1993. Czech ministry report on Julius's friends Joel Barr and Alfred Sarant released to Schneirs

1993-1996. Alexander Vassiliev given access to selected KGB documents

1995. Release of KGB cables decrypted in "Venona" project

1997. Joseph Albright and Marcia Kunstel tell Theodore Hall story in *Bombshell*

1999. Vassiliev transcripts and summaries of KGB cables published

Nov. 1976. Jimmy Carter elected president

1987. *Glasnost* **and** *Perestroika* reforms introduced in USSR by Mikhail Gorbachev

1989. Communist regimes fall in Eastern Europe

1991. Collapse of Soviet Union

1996. UN adopts nuclear test ban treaty

Sept. 2001. World Trade Center attack; President George W. Bush launches "War on Terror"

2001-present. Patriot Act expands government surveillance of U.S.

The Haunted Wood, co-authored by Allen Weinstein

2001. David Greenglass retracts his trial testimony against Ethel In Sam Roberts' *The Brother*

2008. Sobell admits passing nonatomic info

2009. Vassiliev notebooks made public

2009. *Spies* by Harvey Klehr, John Earl Haynes, and Vassiliev is published

citizens and non-citizens

2001-present. U.S. forces in Afghanistan

2002, 2005. U.S. Justice Dept. memos authorize torture of suspected terrorists

2002-present. Suspected terrorists held without trial in U.S. prison at Guantanamo, Cuba

2003-present. U.S. forces in Iraq

PREFACE: A LONG JOURNEY

Miriam Schneir

For fifty years, my husband and colleague Walter Schneir remained a dedicated student of the Rosenberg case. From 1959, when he and I began the research that resulted in our jointly authored book *Invitation to an Inquest* until his sudden death in April 2009 at the age of 81, his fascination with the trial and its broader meanings never flagged. In his career as a writer, Walter authored articles and books dealing with politics, medicine, science, education, and law, and also wrote fiction and poetry—but he always came back to the atom-spy drama that so intrigued him. In his last years he was at work on what he called a "political memoir." It was to be the story of his life, but also of the Rosenberg case, for the two were inextricably intertwined. Chapters from that unfinished memoir form the heart of the present volume.

Over the years, well-meaning friends sometimes wondered aloud why Walter, a man they knew to have wide-ranging interests and a passionate commitment to peace and justice, had chosen to give so much attention to one subject for so many decades. To them, the 1951 prosecution of Julius and Ethel Rosenberg no doubt seemed an event whose significance in the grand scheme of things had gradually faded. But to Walter, the Rosenberg case was like that proverbial grain of sand in which one can see a world. He understood that great legal cases—like those of Dreyfus, Sacco-Vanzetti, Mooney-Billings, the Scottsboro Boys, and the Rosenbergs—embody and illuminate major events and issues of their times. Thus, his research necessarily encompassed the Great Depression, the rise of fascism and communism, the development of the atomic bomb, the Cold War, McCarthyism, anti-Semitism, sexism, the criminal justice system, capital punishment, and much more.

Walter regarded it as a writer's duty to pursue the truth. To do so was, in his view, an endeavor sufficient unto itself, requiring no further justification. Each research breakthrough, each new bit of knowledge, fueled his determination to solve the remaining mysteries of the Rosenberg case. At the end, he was satisfied that he had reached his goal; that he finally knew what had really happened—and why.

• • •

Julius and Ethel Rosenberg, an obscure working-class couple, were catapulted into the limelight when they were arrested in the summer of 1950 and charged with conspiring to transmit secret national defense information to the Soviet Union. At the time of their arrest the Rosenbergs were living with their two young sons in a three-room apartment in New York City's Lower East Side. Like many others who grew up during the Depression, they believed that socialism was the cure for the economic suffering they saw around them, and Julius became a member of the Communist Party. Also arrested that summer and named as a Rosenberg co-conspirator was Morton Sobell, a former engineering classmate of Julius's at the City College of New York (CCNY). All three defendants pleaded not guilty.

The trial of United States versus the Rosenbergs and Sobell opened on March 6, 1951, in New York City's federal courthouse at Foley Square. Outside the imposing neoclassical building with its tall Corinthian columns, Cold War tensions ran high: American soldiers were dying in Korea; Senator Joseph R. McCarthy had launched a crusade to root Communists out of the government; and the Soviet Union's recent test of an atomic device had shown that U.S. cities were vulnerable to attacks like those that had leveled Hiroshima and Nagasaki. In his opening speech to the jury, chief prosecutor Irving Saypol underscored the gravity of the case: The Rosenbergs, he charged, had been able to "steal . . . this one weapon, that might well hold the key to the survival of this nation and means the peace of the world, the atomic bomb." Nothing could have insulated that courtroom from the fears and animosities of the day.

Not surprisingly, the jury voted to convict. Judge Irving R. Kaufman sentenced Sobell to thirty years in prison for passing non-atomic technical information. The Rosenbergs were condemned to death. In passing judgment on the Rosenbergs, Judge Kaufman told them that by putting the A-bomb into the hands of the Cold War enemy years before they would otherwise have had it, "you undoubtedly have altered the course of history to the disadvantage of our country."

The sheer magnitude of the Rosenbergs' alleged crime, plus the severity of the sentence, sparked widespread debate and mass protests. People from many parts of the world raised serious questions about the proceedings. Was there really a discrete "secret" of the atomic bomb, and if so, would it be possible for non-scientists to "steal" it? Could a jury render a just verdict in a trial involving political radicals at a time when the United States was fighting a war against Communist North Korea and China, and anti-Communist sentiment was at fever pitch at home? Had anti-Semitism influenced the verdict? After all, the Rosenbergs and Sobell were Jewish—as were the principal government witnesses, two of the prosecutors (Irving Saypol and his assistant Roy Cohn), and the judge—but there were no Jews on the jury. Finally, there was the matter of the double death penalty. Wasn't the sentence excessive, especially since the theft of atomic information had taken place during a period when Russia was an ally? Some 200,000 pleas for clemency poured into the White House, including from such notables as Pablo Picasso, Jean-Paul Sartre, Albert Einstein, and Pope Pius XII, as well as from the daughter of Alfred Dreyfus and the sister of Bartolomeo Vanzetti. But President Eisenhower refused to grant a stay. Ethel Rosenberg, 37, and Julius Rosenberg, 35, were put to death in the electric chair at Sing Sing Prison in Ossining, New York, on June 19, 1953. Sobell was sent to the federal prison system's harshest facility, Alcatraz penitentiary.

• • •

Walter and I started to research our book just six years after the executions. For two young, independent writers with limited financial resources, to set out to reexamine J. Edgar Hoover's most famous spy case in that benighted period was more than a bit intimidating. Aware that we might be treading on powerful feet, we agreed that it would be best to tell no one what we were working on. We feared that if word got out to the FBI, the agency would find ways to impede our research. Were we being paranoid? As we found out later, we were not being paranoid enough.

The only primary source materials available to us at that early date were the trial transcript and the appeals record. As we studied these documents, we realized that the government's case against the Rosenbergs rested on the testimony of just two people: Ethel's younger brother David Greenglass, a twenty-nine-year-old machinist with a high school education, and his wife Ruth, a typist and homemaker. At the trial, the Greenglasses described two 1945 family-gatherings-cum-espionage-meetings with the Rosenbergs. The prosecution charged that on each of these occasions David, a soldier on furlough in New York, gave Julius secret information relating to the atomic bomb project at Los Alamos, which Ethel then typed up for delivery to the Russians.

But unfortunately, neither incident was amenable to further investigation, since both were said to have taken place in the Rosenbergs' New York City apartment with no outside witness present. However, the Greenglasses also testified to one occasion when David gave information to a person other than Julius at a place other than the Rosenberg home. This episode, we thought, might offer possibilities for follow-up research.

According to the Greenglasses' testimony, a man they now knew to be Philadelphia chemist Harry Gold called at their apartment in Albuquerque, New Mexico, on Sunday morning, June 3, 1945. Ruth had rented the apartment so that her husband, an enlisted man stationed by the Army at nearby Los Alamos, could visit her on weekends. The Greenglasses further testified that Gold introduced himself to them with a password that included the name Julius, and he showed them a piece of a Jello box side that matched a piece Julius Rosenberg had cut and given to them in New York. David gave Gold some handwritten notes and a few rough sketches of high-explosive lens molds, a device David was familiar with from his work at a Los Alamos machine shop. Gold paid the Greenglasses $500.

Harry Gold was the prosecution's chief corroborative witness. Prior to taking the witness stand at the Rosenberg trial, he had already confessed to serving as a spy courier to Klaus Fuchs, a German-born physicist from England who worked at Los Alamos during the war years. Addressing the Rosenberg jury, Gold said that in spring 1945, his Soviet handler, Anatoli Yakovlev, had ordered him to take on an additional mission during his next trip to Santa Fe to see Fuchs. This "extra added attraction," as Gold later referred to it, was a visit to Albuquerque to pick up information from a GI. Gold testified that Yakovlev supplied him with the GI's address, a sealed envelope containing $500, a piece of a card that appeared to be cut from a packaged food of some sort, and the password "I come from Julius." These recognition signals were the only evidence presented at the trial that connected the Rosenbergs—or more accurately, Julius Rosenberg—to a Russian agent. Prosecutor Saypol declared that Harry Gold's testimony had "forged the necessary link in the chain that points indisputably to the guilt of the Rosenbergs."

The prosecution introduced two items of documentary evidence in support of the Greenglass-Gold testimony: a June 3, 1945, Albuquerque Hilton Hotel registration card in Gold's name and bank records indicating that the Greenglasses had deposited $400 to their account on June 4.

Early on in our research, Walter and I learned that Harry Gold's attorneys had interviewed Gold extensively in preparation for his sentencing hearing and had recorded the conversations. We requested access to these recordings plus any written material Gold had given them. The attorneys conveyed our request to their client, who was then serving a thirty-year prison term. For reasons we never ascertained, Gold instructed them to grant us "carte blanche." Only a handful of people— representatives of the FBI and of the Senate Internal Security subcommittee and one well-known journalist—had previously been allowed to listen to the recordings. Indeed, their very

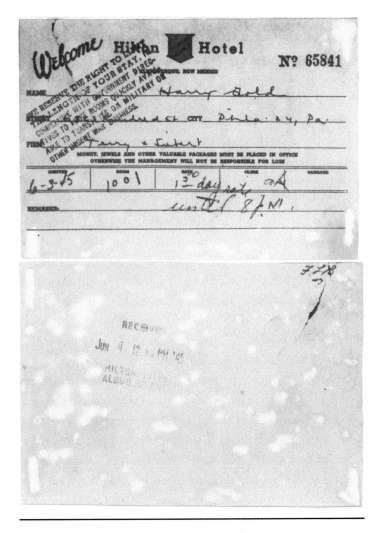

Harry Gold's June 3, 1945, Albuquerque Hilton Hotel registration card was a prosecution exhibit at the Rosenberg trial. As pointed out in Invitation to an Inquest, *the card has several major defects: a photostat was introduced into evidence instead of the original document; it was not properly initialed and dated by the FBI agents who retrieved it; and the date-time stamp on the reverse, which is supposed to show the check-in time, is incorrect (June 4 rather than June 3). In addition, a handwriting expert who examined the card expressed "some very real doubts" about the genuineness of the portion filled out by the clerk. U.S. Attorney Irving R. Saypol told the jury that the June card established the "veracity of David and Ruth Greenglass and of Harry Gold"; however, the validity of the card itself remains open to question.*

existence was nearly unknown. For two relative neophytes, it was a stupendous research coup.

What we were most eager to hear on the recordings was how Gold had described the June 3 meeting to his lawyers before he could have had any knowledge of what the Greenglasses would say about it. Gold made no reference to the episode in any of the initial interviews. Finally, just one day before the FBI questioned David Greenglass, . . . Gold alluded to picking up information from a GI in Albuquerque. When his attorney interrupted to inquire if he had used a recognition sign with the soldier, we waited with bated breath for Gold's answer. To our astonishment, he said nothing about a piece of card from a packaged food container, nor did he mention the name Julius. Instead, he said that he thought he had used a password that "involved the name of a man and was something on the order of Bob sent me or Benny sent me or John sent me or something like that." Incredibly, the "necessary link" that connected the Rosenbergs to Gold's Russian handler Anatoli Yakovlev was missing.

As we pursued the story of the June 3 rendezvous, we came up with evidence that undermined key elements of the neatly meshing Greenglass-Gold testimony. Especially disturbing were the circumstances surrounding Harry Gold's Albuquerque Hilton Hotel registration card. After extensive research, we became convinced that the card was not produced in the ordinary course of the hotel's business. Moreover, the prosecution's contention that David Greenglass had memorized the "secret" of the atomic bomb and carried it out of Los Alamos in his head seemed to us an inherently preposterous claim—one that reflected, more than anything else, the ignorance and fear that pervaded the early years of the atomic age. Based on the cumulative weight of all our findings, we ultimately concluded that Julius and Ethel Rosenberg were not only "unjustly convicted, they were punished for a crime that never occurred." Doubleday published *Invitation to an Inquest* in 1965, but that was by no means the end of the matter.

An appeal launched in 1966 by attorneys representing the Rosenbergs' co-defendant Morton Sobell made use of some of our discoveries. Although the appeal was unsuccessful, it did succeed in forcing the prosecution to make public for the first time Exhibit 8, which had been impounded at the trial and kept secret ever since. The exhibit consisted of a sketch and explanatory material that David Greenglass had prepared after his arrest for use at the trial and which, he testified, was a facsimile of a drawing he had turned over to Julius Rosenberg in the latter's apartment during his September 1945 furlough. A number of leading scientists who examined the drawing— which was labeled "not to scale"—contested the prosecution's claim that Exhibit 8 represented, in Roy Cohn's words, "the atom bomb itself." Physicist Philip Morrison, a former Los Alamos employee, ridiculed the sketch as "confused and imprecise," no more than a "caricature" of the actual device, while scientist Henry Linschitz, who also had worked on the bomb project, called Greenglass's data "garbled." He commented: "It is not possible in any technologically useful way to condense the results of a two-billion-dollar development effort into a diagram, drawn by a high-school graduate machinist on a single sheet of paper."

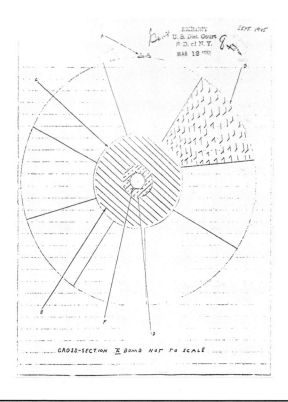

CROSS-SECTION ☓ BOMB NOT TO SCALE

Greenglass testified: "I have A, which points to two detonators, each mold. Each high explosive lens, there were 36 of them, that I have pointed to as B had two detonators on them; that is, two detonators connected to capacitators which were charged by suitable apparatus and was set to go off by a switch that would throw all 72 condensers at once. . . . And beneath the high explosive lens there was C, . . . a beryllium plastic sphere, which is a shield for the h.e., the high explosive. Then I have E, which is the plutonium itself, which is fissionable material. That is also a sphere. Inside that sphere is a D, is beryllium. Inside the beryllium there are conical shaped holes F, marked F.

"Now, the beryllium shield protects the high explosive from the radiation of the plutonium. . . . At the time of the discharge of the condensers the high explosive lens implode giving a concentric implosion to the plutonium sphere. . . . This in turn does the same to the beryllium, and the beryllium is the neutron source which ejects neutrons into the plutonium, . . . and nuclear fission takes place. . . . "

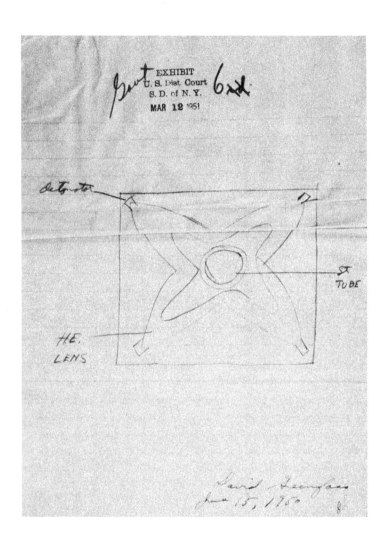

Government Exhibit 6

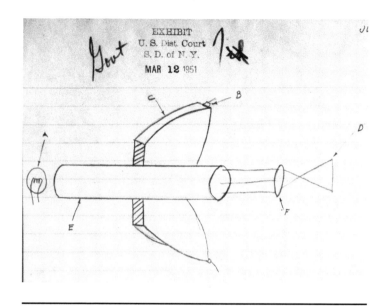

Government Exhibit 7

These sketches were drawn by David Greenglass in 1950 and 1951
in preparation for the Rosenberg trial. Greenglass testified that they
were replicas of sketches he had turned over to Harry Gold in June
1945. Regarding Exhibit 6, he testified: "I showed a high-explosive
lens mold. I showed the way it would look with this high explosive
in it with the detonators on, and I showed the steel tube in the middle
which would be exploded [sic, should be imploded] by this lens mold."
Exhibit 7, he said, depicted "the lens mold set up for an experiment."
He described the lettered parts as follows: "A is the light source"; E
"shows a camera set up to take a picture of this light source"; C "is
a cross-section of the high explosive lens"; B is a detonator; F is a
camera lens; and the film D shows a picture of the implosion." An
expert technical witness testifying for the prosecution observed that the
sketches were "rough" and did not show "dimensions," but they did
"illustrate the important principle involved."

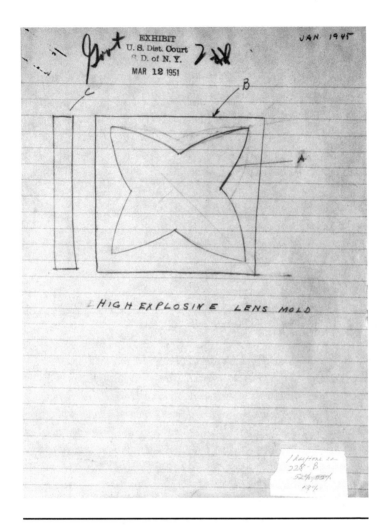

Government Exhibit 2
David Greenglass testified that he gave a replica of this sketch of
a high-explosive lens mold to Julius Rosenberg in January 1945.
Greenglass identified the parts as follows: "A refers to the curve of the
lens; B is the frame; C shows approximately how wide it is. . . . It is
a four-leaf clover design like; it looks something similar."

For a new edition of *Invitation to an Inquest*, Walter and I prepared a chapter detailing the 1966 legal action and its disposition in the courts. The chapter ended by pointing out that "the questions raised by the Sobell appeal remain unanswered; the secret files of the Department of Justice remain locked."

• • •

The files stayed locked until public outrage over the Watergate scandal unsealed them. Responding to urgent calls for greater transparency, outgoing Attorney General Elliot Richardson ordered long-secret government papers opened to historians and other researchers. In a December 1974 *New York Times* op-ed piece, Walter wrote that Richardson's directive had "promised answers to many questions about F.B.I. activities during the McCarthy era." However, he added, seventeen months had since gone by, and the agency still had not released a single page from the Rosenberg files. The next year the Rosenbergs' sons, Michael and Robert Meeropol (their adoptive name), inaugurated a lawsuit under a newly strengthened Freedom of Information Act.

In the seventies and eighties, a number of American writers and artists were moved to take a new look at the Rosenberg case and the repressive era that had spawned it. *Inquest*, by Donald Freed, a play based on our book, was produced on Broadway in 1970; directed by Alan Schneider, it starred Anne Jackson as Ethel, George Grizzard as Julius, and James Whitmore as the chief defense attorney. Writers E. L. Doctorow and Robert Coover created fictional versions of the case in their novels *The Book of Daniel* (1971) and *The Public Burning* (1976). A ninety-minute documentary by Alvin H. Goldstein, "The Unquiet Death of Julius and Ethel Rosenberg," was produced for public television in Washington, D.C. First aired in 1974, it later was published in book form. In a 1980 poem titled "For Ethel Rosenberg," Adrienne Rich wrote that the memory of Ethel had sunk into her soul, "A weight of sadness / I can hardly register how deep. . . ." A Bob Dylan song, "Julius and Ethel," recorded in 1983, included the verses, "Now that they are gone, you know, the truth it can come out / They were never proven guilty beyond a reasonable doubt"; and, "Eisenhower was president, Senator Joe was King / Long as you didn't say nothing you could say anything." Each verse ended with the refrain, "Julius and Ethel, Julius and Ethel." In a powerful mixed-media work titled "Needs of the State," artist Sue Coe portrayed a figure labeled "Truth" strapped into an electric chair. Julius and Ethel Rosenberg stand on either side of the chair, while in a gallery high above the death chamber, witnesses to the execution—including J. Edgar Hoover, Judge Irving R. Kaufman, and Torquemada—prepare to pull the switch.

Writing a bit more than thirty years after the executions, playwright Arthur Miller recalled hearing on his car radio that the Rosenbergs had exhausted all legal options and would be put to death that very evening. Still, he wrote, he had been confident "something or someone would intervene at the last minute and stop it, call it a bad dream. . . . Where was Eisenhower?" he asked. "Where was anybody who did not have career interest in an execution, or an ideological passion to hunt these two down? Where was justice, cool and dispassion-ate?" But of course, the execution did take place—indeed, was moved ahead to just before sundown so as not to desecrate the Jewish Sabbath. That night, at the New York City per-formance of *The Crucible*, Miller's drama based on the Salem witch trials, the audience did not applaud at the end of the play but stood to observe a minute of silence.[1]

The Meeropol brothers' extraordinarily protracted Free-dom of Information suit to obtain government documents was still in progress when the fourth American edition of *Invitation to an Inquest* was published by Pantheon Books in 1983. Walter and I noted in the new edition that the Meeropol litiga-tion to date had compelled the FBI to release a total of about 160,000 pages, while other federal agencies had released tens of thousands more. Although words, paragraphs, and even entire pages were censored, the documents nonetheless yield-ed fascinating information.

On a personal level, Walter and I learned from the FBI files that it had taken the Bureau a little over a year to find out about our research endeavors (the telephone of a known left-ist we interviewed was apparently being listened in on). From that point on, federal agents followed the progress of our book more closely and with far keener interest than did our editor at Doubleday. The FBI's Schneir investigation, we discovered, was set in motion in 1961 in response to a direct order from J. Edgar Hoover himself. To keep abreast of our activities, the Bureau made use of telephone taps and mail covers and also contacted various of our acquaintances, neighbors, work as-sociates, and other potential sources of information. As the scope of our research widened, so too did the FBI's surveillance of our activities. Week after week, Washington headquarters ordered additional Bureau offices to open files on the Schneirs: Minneapolis, Newark, Los Angeles, San Antonio, Albuquerque, San Francisco, Chicago, Miami, Omaha.

In a report he wryly titled "How I Became a Public Enemy," Walter described our FBI dossier. "What crime had I committed to merit such scrutiny?" he asked. "It was a heinous one indeed. I was writing a book on a topic about which Mr. Hoover was obviously wary: the Rosenberg Case."

Our files further revealed that after we had submitted the completed manuscript of *Invitation to an Inquest* to Doubleday in 1964, the FBI had asked to see pre-publication galleys. However, the times they were a-changing, and our mainstream publishers were not easily cowed. They consulted us, and when we demurred, they denied the request. Later, FBI agents interfered with our efforts to promote the book by trying to intimidate radio and TV hosts who had invited one or both of us to speak.

By 1967, the FBI had been dogging our footsteps for six years. At some point during those years, the investigation had taken a bizarre turn. Walter explained:

The title on the file designated for me by Hoover—
"Miscellaneous-Information Concerning"—had been
expanded. A single, powerfully incriminating word
had been added: "Espionage." And whereas previously reports on me had been passed on to the Domestic

Intelligence Division, now they were directed to the James Bond world of international intrigue, the FBI's Soviet Section. From an author writing a book about accused spies, I had become an accused spy myself.

Ludicrously, our names were added to the Bureau's list of individuals who might pose a danger to the president of the United States. More ominously, we were placed on an index of persons the FBI could detain in the event of a national emergency. Walter commented that if we were arrested, we would be in good company: "Among the thousand or so other Americans whose Section A Reserve Index cards were secreted in the recesses of the United States Department of Justice were Martin Luther King, Jr., poet John Ciardi, and Mario Savio, the eloquent conscience of the Berkeley Free Speech Movement."

Far more significant than our personal FBI files were those that disclosed the step-by-step process by which the Greenglasses had incriminated Julius. In David's first FBI statement—which he signed at 1:30 a.m. on June 16, 1950—he not only confessed his own guilt but, seemingly unwittingly, ascribed an active role in the conspiracy to his wife. Julius was mentioned in David's initial statement almost as an afterthought.

When the FBI first interviewed Ruth Greenglass, she denied everything. But with David in prison and she herself in imminent danger of arrest, she quickly recognized the wisdom of a less hazardous path: cooperation. In the next few weeks, Ruth, followed by David, fleshed out the story, shifting much of the blame for their actions onto their brother-in-law. Julius was taken into custody on July 17.

The inculpation of Ethel evolved more slowly. The FBI files show that she remained for months a marginal figure in the Greenglasses' confessions. Nonetheless, she was arrested in August and denied bail. As late as February 1951, just a month before the opening of the trial, an assistant U.S. attorney from New York City still had to admit, "The case is not too strong against Mrs. Rosenberg." This inconvenient fact did not deter him from telling the dignitaries attending a special session of the Joint Congressional Committee on Atomic Energy, "The only thing that will break this man Rosenberg is the prospect of . . . getting the [electric] chair, plus that if we can convict his wife . . . that combination may serve to make this fellow disgorge." Not one member of that august assembly objected to his *Alice-in-Wonderland*-like pronouncement of "Sentence first—verdict afterward"; nor did anyone point out that the Rosenbergs were entitled to a presumption of innocence. In fact, Ethel remained incarcerated for the rest of her life, a sacrifice to the government's vain hope that the suffering of his wife and two young sons would persuade Julius to confess and name confederates.

In the fall of 1983, Mark Kuchment, a Russian historian of science who had emigrated to the United States, announced that he had discovered what had become of two of Julius Rosenberg's friends, Joel Barr and Alfred Sarant. Both men had vanished without a trace in 1950, at about the time of Greenglass's arrest. At the trial, prosecutors had labeled them *in absentia* members of a Rosenberg spy ring.

Now Kuchment convincingly showed that two brilliantly successful Soviet scientists known as Josef Berg and Filip Staros were none other than Barr and Sarant. Berg and Staros had arrived in the Soviet Union in the mid-1950s from Czechoslovakia and had made important contributions to the Russian microelectronics industry. Kuchment's discovery was made public in the *New York Times* on the morning of the day Walter and I were scheduled to debate the authors of a new book on the Rosenberg case, in New York City's Town Hall.[2] We argued in the debate that the disappearance of two openly radical individuals like Barr and Sarant at the height of the McCarthy era might have had no relationship to espionage.

• • •

The political upheavals of the 1990s presented previously un-dreamed-of research opportunities to historians of the Cold War. Although Sarant/Staros was deceased, Julius's old friend, college classmate, and Communist Party comrade Joel Barr/Josef Berg was alive and well in Leningrad. Walter wrote to Barr requesting an interview. Now free to communicate with people outside the Soviet bloc for the first time in four decades, Barr responded, and in October 1990, he visited the United States. Walter spent a good deal of time with Barr during that first whirlwind trip and afterward jotted down a few fast impressions of the spirited 73-year-old: "intelligent, energetic, outrageous, amusing, fabulous, a risk-taker." As we came to know Barr better, we found him to be both a charming companion and a thorough scoundrel.

In November 1990, we flew to Prague. We had arranged to meet Barr there, but the principal purpose of our visit was to learn more about his and Sarant's life in Czechoslovakia in the fifties. It had been just a year since the popular uprising known as the Velvet Revolution had toppled the nation's Communist regime, and candles and flowers were massed at the foot of the memorial to Saint Wenceslaus in celebration of the people's victory. With some difficulty, we wrangled appointments with officials at the once powerful Czech Communist Party as well as at the Federal Ministry of the Interior. The CP functionary with whom we met was pessimistic, but he agreed to check for Barr/Berg and Sarant/Staros in their files. He informed us a few days later that there was no record of either man. At the Interior Ministry, a young official, Jan Frolik, promised to make a thorough search of the Ministry's archives. More than a year later, after we had given up all hope of hearing from him, we learned that he was holding information for us.

Frolik's report said that Joel Barr, alias Josef Berg, arrived in Czechoslovakia in June 1950 on a British passport and lived there for five years. Berg's first job was at an electronics firm. Then, "according to the order of the Minister of Defence and at the recommendation of the central Committee of the Party and personally Mr. [Rudolf] Slansky, [he worked] at the Army Technical Institute . . . on secret projects connected with anti-aircraft-raid defence. He was the protégé (under the protection) of the director of the Institute." Alfred Sarant, alias Filip Staros, reached Czechoslovakia in 1951. He too was employed at the Army Institute. In 1953, both men took jobs at another technical facility, and two years later both went to the Soviet Union. Frolik's overall conclusion was that "Barr/Berg has most definitely not been a usual political émigré." He based this opinion on a number of factors, among them that neither he nor Sarant/Staros was followed by the secret police, "as was usual with other political émigrés." He also remarked on the high status of Berg's protectors and the speed with which he was granted permission to work on secret projects.

Walter and I were taken aback to see the powerful Czech politician Rudolf Slansky named as one of Barr/Berg's protectors, for we knew that not long after Barr's arrival in Czechoslovakia, Slansky himself was in need of a protector. In spite of his high rank in the ruling Czech Communist Party, Slansky was placed under arrest in the fall of 1951, and a year later, he and thirteen co-defendants—eleven of whom, like him, were of Jewish origin—were accused of conspiring against the state. After a show trial whose blatant anti-Semitism shocked people around the world, Slansky and ten others were sentenced to death and executed. We realized that Barr/Berg, who was also Jewish, would under normal circumstances have come under suspicion. Yet despite his guardian's fall from grace, he was allowed to continue doing secret work.

Walter sent a thank-you letter to Frolik. "Of course the information on Berg and Staros is not what we would have hoped," he wrote. "But, as we told you at the time of our meeting, we were interested in learning the truth—whatever it might be." In a personal memo to himself, Walter noted his tentative conclusion: "Barr and Sarant probably had close ties to Soviet intelligence."

We wanted to give Barr a chance to respond to the implications of Frolik's report, and when he was again in New York that spring, we invited him to our home. After dinner, we summarized Frolik's main points. Barr became enraged, said we were accusing him of lying, and stormed from the house. Despite the sound and fury, we were not convinced of his sincerity, and further research focusing on Sarant/Staros's experiences in Czechoslovakia and the Soviet Union served only to reinforce our suspicions. But did it necessarily mean that Julius Rosenberg was a spy? That question was still up in the air.

In 1991, Walter obtained a copy of a two-part article from the Russian magazine *New Times*. The author, an associate of the public relations office of the KGB, had written, "The time has now come to disclose what has remained a mystery for over fifty years and what the American and British intelligence services have never found out, for all their pains."* The author then revealed that a U.S.-born woman named Lona Cohen, aka Helen Kroger, had helped the Soviet Union obtain classified information from Los Alamos during World War II. Lona was already an infamous Soviet spy, for she and her husband Morris Cohen had been convicted in 1961 of espionage activities in England and sentenced to twenty years in prison. However, despite the KGB man's swaggering tone, we had to admit that his claim that Lona had also been an atom-spy in the United States during the forties, if true, was news.

The *New Times* piece was one of several indications that aging KGB stalwarts were eager to tell the world about their espionage feats. To take advantage of this situation, Walter developed mutually helpful relationships with a number of

---

* The Soviet spy agencies had a number of different names, but the more familiar KGB is generally used here.

journalists and other individuals interested in Cold War history. One of these contacts—Svetlana Chervonnaya, a scholar affiliated with the Russian Institute of USA and Canada—notified him that a former KGB operative named Anatoli Yatskov had boasted in a Russian TV documentary that while stationed at the Soviet consulate in New York during World War II, he was assigned to handle atomic espionage. Svetlana also reported that Yatskov had referred to Lona Cohen and Harry Gold as two of his couriers. Walter soon got hold of a copy of the Russian documentary. Based on details of the former KGB agent's story as well as his physical appearance, Walter surmised that Yatskov was in all likelihood Anatoli Yakovlev, the man Harry Gold named at the Rosenberg trial as the Soviet contact who had sent him to the Greenglasses with the Julius password and the piece of a Jello box.

Walter shared his theory with *Washington Post* reporter Michael Dobbs, who interviewed Yatskov in Moscow in October 1992. Dobbs sent Walter a transcript of the interview, which included the following interchange:

> Q. Walter Schneir thinks you were Anatoli Antonovich Yakovlev.
> A. [speaking English] Yes, I used the name Yakovlev but I had no connection with the Rosenbergs. I worked under the name of Yakovlev. I did not know them [the Rosenbergs] and I had no connection with them, but I happened to be mentioned in the same indictment with them.

Q. Why?

A. Because the trial did not begin with Rosenbergs. It began from Gold and Gold was a messenger who went to Los Alamos and brought back materials to me. . . .

Q. As far as Rosenbergs were concerned. . . .

A. On the Rosenbergs, let's agree this way . . . I only know what was written about them in newspapers, what was in the court proceedings.

Yatskov's denial of any personal connection to or knowledge of the Rosenbergs was at the least equivocal. As for his earlier claim that Lona Cohen had carried A-bomb data out of Los Alamos and delivered it to him, interesting though it was, it failed to answer what for us was a crucial question: What did she know about the Rosenbergs?

Walter began to lay the groundwork for a trip to Russia. He learned that the Cohens were in Moscow, where they had lived since leaving England in 1969 in a prisoner exchange with the USSR, and he addressed a letter to Lona asking to meet her. To his surprise, she neither refused nor acquiesced, but instead suggested a bit of old-fashioned horse-trading. If Walter could locate members of her family in the United States, she told him, she would agree to meet with him. Previous attempts to find Lona's relatives by her intelligence-agency colleagues and other Russian officials had ended in failure, and she probably assumed that Walter would be equally unsuccessful. But armed with the names, birth dates, and last known addresses of Lona's eight sisters and two brothers, he soon tracked down all her surviving relatives. A sister, Ginger—since remarried,

with a new last name, and living in a different state—was en-
thusiastic about the prospect of a reunion with her long-lost
sibling. Walter advised Lona that he had found her sister, but
he held back Ginger's whereabouts until the quid pro quo they
had agreed upon was officially approved. The authorization
came, and after Ginger had completed her visit to Moscow, it
was Walter's turn.

Walter was quickly apprised of the fact that in the former
Soviet Union access to information was strictly on a pay-to-
play basis. He later reported:

> When I arrived in Moscow on a research trip in late
> 1992, I found a message waiting for me from Igor Pre-
> lin, who until the collapse of the Soviet Union the
> previous year had been a high KGB officer. In the
> new Russia, Prelin had neatly transformed himself
> from intelligence agent to literary agent. He now rep-
> resented a stable of down at the heels retired spies
> who had agreed to disclose their medal-winning ex-
> ploits in exchange for cash on the barrelhead. The
> entrepreneurial Prelin left word that he could arrange
> an interview for me with one of his clients, the aged
> and ailing Leonid Kvasnikov, who during World War
> II had served the KGB in New York City in the key
> post of chief of scientific and technical espionage. The
> price was $500. That was a hefty sum in the topsy-
> turvy Russia then, nearly the equivalent in rubles to
> what my host, Svetlana Chervonnaya, received for
> her entire yearly salary as a scholar in a prestigious
> Moscow think tank. Fresh from affluent America, I

was perhaps rather strait-laced about the ethics of paying for interviews but also, I think, justifiably dubious about the accuracy of tales I might be told by people whose sole motive for talking to me would be the Yankee dollar. I declined Prelin's offer.

Accompanied by Svetlana, Walter conferred with several members of the new Russian intelligence service. Citing the interests of history, he made a strong pitch for access to KGB files, but since he was unable to offer a substantial economic incentive, he made no headway. Nonetheless, he did receive permission to interview not only Lona Cohen, then gravely ill in a Moscow hospital, but also Yakovlev/Yatskov, who was currently being treated in another hospital.

Walter interviewed Lona and Morris Cohen several times. Although Lona was extremely grateful to him for arranging a last visit with her sister, she was desperately sick (she died a month later) and tired quickly. Moreover, she remained to the end a disciplined spy for whom secrecy came more naturally than candor. Still, she did confirm that she had gone on at least two missions to New Mexico for Yatskov and had picked up information from a young scientist there, a man since identified as Theodore Hall. She asserted that she never met or had any knowledge of the Rosenbergs.

Yatskov, too, was cautious about what he was prepared to reveal. He reiterated essentially what he had previously told the *Washington Post* reporter. When Walter asked him who had set up the June 3, 1945, meeting between the Greenglasses and Gold in Albuquerque, he did not respond. Finally, he offered that if the Rosenbergs' sons came to see him in the spring, he would tell them the whole story. But in the spring, Yatskov too was dead.

• • •

In the summer of 1995, the U.S. National Security Agency (NSA) released translations of forty-five Soviet intelligence cables dealing with atomic espionage during World War II. These messages were among some 2,200 intercepted by the U.S. Army's Signal Intelligence Service (a forerunner of the NSA) and painstakingly decoded in a highly secret government program called Venona. The Venona project began in 1943 and lasted for several decades. But according to the NSA, "Almost all of the KGB messages between Moscow and New York and Moscow and Washington of 1944 and 1945 that could be broken at all were broken, to a greater or lesser degree, between 1947 and 1952."[3] In other words, most of the relevant Venona translations were available to the U.S. government before the 1951 Rosenberg-Sobell trial, and nearly all of them before the executions. Although the existence of "secret evidence" in the Rosenberg case had long been rumored, the release of the cables came as a complete surprise to most Americans, including to many members of the U.S. intelligence community.

Venona presented a number of snares to trip up incautious researchers. For example, the documents are replete with gaps where the cryptanalysts were unable to decipher the code; there is no way to verify the accuracy of the decoded texts; nearly all the messages are second- or even third-hand reports (that is, as told to Russian handlers by U.S. sources and then conveyed to Moscow); those Russian agents fortunate enough to be stationed in the United States during the war (and eager to remain) had motive to exaggerate their recruiting and information-gathering achievements to superiors back home; and lastly, since many of the individuals mentioned in the documents were referred to solely by code names, their identities had to be surmised based on context.

Notwithstanding these caveats, when Walter and I read the pertinent Venona cables, it was immediately evident to us that Julius Rosenberg, code-named "Antenna" and later "Liberal," had worked as a spy for the Soviet Union. When put together with everything else we had learned in recent years, Venona left no room for doubt that Julius had persuaded friends and political comrades to give technical data from their jobs to the Russians. We reported in an editorial in *The Nation* that although the government's case against Julius had relied upon fabricated evidence, "the Venona messages reveal that during World War II Julius ran a spy ring composed of young fellow Communists, including friends and college classmates whom he had recruited. The group gave technical data from their jobs—information on radar and airplanes is mentioned in the documents. Julius passed this material on to the Soviets." We noted, in addition, that the Venona messages "implicate the American Communist Party in recruitment of party members for espionage."

On the other hand, we pointed out that the decrypts do not confirm the principal elements of the atomic conspiracy.

In fact, "the Venona documents corroborate only a relatively minor role in atomic espionage for Julius, one that occurred as a result of the serendipitous stationing at Los Alamos of his brother-in-law, David Greenglass, a soldier." Moreover, Venona absolves Ethel Rosenberg. A transmission from New York to the Moscow KGB center identifies her without a code name as "Liberal's wife . . . Ethel"; and it unambiguously states that she "knows about her husband's work," but on account of ill health, she herself "does not work." We acknowledged in closing, "We know that our account will be painful news for many people, as it is for us."

A letter to the editor published in *The Nation* urged us to apologize for having mistakenly defended the Rosenbergs for so many years, but we declined to issue the requested mea culpa. "We are not ashamed that we chose to write a history of the early atomic age focusing on the Rosenberg case at a time when the subject was verboten in the mass media," we wrote in response. "Nor that through years of research we uncovered irrefutable proof of fabricated evidence. Nor that we fought hard with many others to free Morton Sobell from a barbaric thirty-year sentence." We ended our answer with a phrase Walter used again in one of the chapters below: "No regrets. No apologies."

A year after the Venona release, Walter and I found ourselves in a hotel suite in downtown Manhattan conducting the first American interview with retired KGB colonel Alexander Feklisov. Feklisov had staked a claim to a leading role in the Rosenberg affair when he approached Svetlana Chervonnaya at Yatskov's funeral, introduced himself, and indicated that he had been Julius Rosenberg's espionage superior in the United States for a couple of years during the forties. Like other ex-KGBers, Colonel Feklisov was writing a book. He wanted Svetlana to help him, but after working with him for a time and double-checking what he told her, Svetlana concluded that his stories were "like those of old-time hunters and fishers: their prey and fish are always fantastic."

Now, Feklisov was about to make his public debut in the United States on a Discovery channel TV documentary, and we had been asked to interview him. Although the program's producers probably hoped we would attest to their star's bona fides, we were unable to disentangle what he knew first-hand from what he had since read or been told. In the end, we could neither endorse nor refute Feklisov's detailed account. Walter subsequently wrote an editorial for *The Nation* entitled "Tales from the K.G.B." in which he emphasized the importance of documentary proof in such instances. He pointed out:

> Feklisov's story highlights a problem that has bedeviled students of America's cold war spy cases. Despite promises by the Russian government, to date few if any relevant K.G.B. documents have been made public. Into the void come the K.G.B. storytellers, strangers with mixed motives offering us piecemeal instant history. Some of their narratives may be true, some a pack of lies; still others are half-truths embellished with newsworthy details that provide commercial currency.

• • •

Walter never had any second thoughts about the validity of his life's work, for he understood that the writing of history, particularly contemporary history, is a process that involves constant revision as new information is uncovered. Moreover, he remained convinced that our original conclusion—that both Rosenbergs, but especially Ethel Rosenberg, were unjustly convicted of having stolen the secret of the atomic bomb—was correct. Indeed, in the era of 9/11, he was more certain than ever that the Rosenberg case provided an instructive example of how easily the justice system can be corrupted by fear of dissident ideas.

Browsing among Walter's voluminous notes, I came across an outline he had prepared showing the scores of research leads, some fruitful, some not, his study of the Rosenberg case had led him to follow over the years. In the midst of this barebones accounting, he had suddenly interjected an exuberant exclamation: "It's been quite a journey!"

What follows is his story of the end of that journey.

ONE

A Mysterious Date: December 27, 1945

Only a few years ago, I would have been writing *finis* here to my search for truth in the Rosenberg case. This might have been the place for the observation that we now knew all we were ever likely to about the affair. But to borrow a phrase from my friend Grace Paley, there have been enormous changes at the last minute. Changes that have not yet been understood, even by those who inadvertently brought them to light. For when we first encounter a discovery that contradicts accepted beliefs, we often fail to grasp the implications of what we are seeing. But I am getting ahead of my story.

• • •

It all began with a phone call from Michael Meeropol, the elder son of Julius and Ethel Rosenberg, soon after the publication in 1997 of the book *Bombshell*, by Joseph Albright and Marcia Kunstel. Michael was disturbed about some new material concerning his parents' case that he had found mentioned in the source notes of *Bombshell*, and he wanted my opinion about it.[4]

As it happened, I had just started to read the book. Its main focus is on Theodore Hall, the young Harvard-educated physicist who while working at Los Alamos during World War II passed information on the atomic bomb to the Russians. But the book also deals with other atomic-espionage cases, including that of the Rosenbergs.

The authors of *Bombshell* are seasoned journalists, highly skilled, who have won frequent recognition for their work. But in addition to their own ingenuity and perseverance, they had one other advantage: money. Albright is the scion of a famous American publishing family, and he and his co-author were able to mount a prodigious research effort.

For their investigation, Albright and Kunstel enlisted a team of six researchers in the United States, and they themselves traveled to England several times to interview Hall and his wife. But the research to which Michael was referring in his phone call was done in Russia, where the authors spent several years as Moscow correspondents for the Cox newspapers.

In their own words: "To fill in the rest of the story, we have relied heavily on Russian intelligence and Ministry of

Atomic Energy documents that briefly became available to researchers in Moscow during the post-perestroika period of 1991–1993, but that have since been reclassified and locked away by Russian authorities." Inasmuch as the authors began their book project in fall 1994, after what they claim was a brief open period, it is not obvious how they managed to gain access to these secret "Russian intelligence and Ministry of Atomic Energy documents." Suffice it to say that they did. Quite likely both their journalistic acumen and their financial resources played a part. Fortunately, they have provided some useful details about their sources in copious back-of-the-book notes.

As Michael described for me the new material that had captured his attention, I suddenly realized what an astonishing find the authors of *Bombshell* had made. They had learned that the original spy reports on the atomic bomb project received by Soviet intelligence agents decades ago are still in existence in an archive at the Russian Ministry of Atomic Energy. While the authors did not secure access to these original spy reports, they did obtain copies of a number of inventory records that describe some of the material that is stored in this unique archive.

According to Albright and Kunstel, the inventory records they procured disclose that in the period after Hiroshima, which occurred on August 6, 1945, Soviet intelligence received three separate reports on the American atomic bomb project: The first report probably contains material from Theodore Hall and possibly some other still-unknown person, and the second seems to be from Klaus Fuchs. As for the third, identified as "document No. 464," Albright and Kunstel comment: "This one corresponds to what Greenglass confessed he handed to Julius Rosenberg in September 1945."

Thus, document No. 464 appears to corroborate David Greenglass's trial testimony that in September 1945 he gave to Julius Rosenberg a sketch and accompanying explanatory material of what Roy Cohn dramatically described in court as "the atom bomb itself." Of course, Michael understood all too well that the September episode had been central to the rationale used to justify the executions of his mother and father. And he was, no doubt, hoping against hope that I might have some alternative interpretation of document No. 464 that would not link it to David.

I suggested to Michael that he obtain from Albright and Kunstel a copy of any inventory records they had relating to document No. 464. He informed me that he had already done so and agreed to fax to me whatever he had received from them. The records that arrived consisted of two pages in Russian, the first a transmittal memo and the second a brief two-paragraph abstract, or synopsis, of the original report that is kept in the archive.

Even with my rudimentary knowledge of Russian, I was able to give Michael a quick answer. The abstract of the spy report bore a telltale sign that connected it unmistakably with David Greenglass: a reference to thirty-six high-explosive lenses in the atomic bomb. The figure "thirty-six" is an error that Greenglass committed consistently both in his statements to the FBI and in his trial testimony. The actual early model of the plutonium A-bomb had thirty-two lenses. Furthermore, the abstract mentioned that the thirty-six lenses were "five-sided," another detail that tied the report to Greenglass, who had mistakenly told the FBI that all thirty-six lenses were "pentagonal shaped." (In fact, twenty of the lenses were hexagon-shaped and twelve were pentagon-shaped.) I had to inform Michael that I felt certain that David Greenglass was the source for the spy report, identified as document No. 464, in the Russian Ministry of Atomic Energy archive.

But not until later, when I had gotten a competent translation, was I alerted to the fact that the material Michael had sent me also contained some wholly new clues about his parents' case, clues that were both fascinating and baffling. The transmittal memo accompanying the spy report had been sent from Vsevolod Merkulov, who as head of the Ministry for State Security was in charge of foreign intelligence, to Lavrenty Beria, chief of the secret police of the Soviet Union and the overseer of that nation's entire atomic bomb program. Merkulov noted in his memo that he was sending Beria a fourteen-page report in English "on the construction of an atomic bomb" and a sample of "an electrodetonator of the bomb." The report and sample had been "obtained by secret agents" and pouched from New York. The memo was dated "27 December 1945." (For reproductions of the memo and the abstract of the report, along with a translation of their texts, see pp. 56–59.)

What was the meaning of the date December 27, 1945? I was stumped. And I found myself no closer to a solution when I carefully reviewed what I knew at that point: In August and September 1945, KGB foreign intelligence agents

To Comrade L.P. Beria

The NKGB of the USSR is sending herewith materials in English on the construction of an atom bomb, as well as an example of the body of an electrodetonator of the bomb, which was obtained by secret agents.

Attachment: 14-page text and 1 sample of the body

(V. Merkulov)

27 December 1945

8603/shch

Post office no. 8 1945
from New York

4 copies sent

1 to addressee
2 C-t NKGB USSR
3 & 4 1st Dept. of NKGB

Bakhmetkov, 11th division

Russian Ministry of Atomic Energy Document No. 464
Transmittal memo, Vsevolod Merkulov to Lavrenti Beria, December 27, 1945

Товарищу БЕРИЯ Л.П.

НКГБ СССР при этом направляет материал на английском языке по конструкции атомной бомбы, а также образец корпуса электродетонатора бомбы, полученные агентурным путем.

ПРИЛОЖЕНИЕ: по тексту на 14 листах и 1 образец корпуса.

(В. МЕРКУЛОВ)

"27" декабря 1945 г.

8608/м

отп. 4 экз.

1 — в адрес
2 — С-т НКГБ СССР
3-4 — 1 Упр. НКГБ СССР

исп. Рахметков, 11 отдел

Notes on the Construction of an Atom Bomb
Description of the Construction of an "Implosion Bomb"

A. *Detonator:*   This part of the bomb has two wires leading to 2 points of detonation (there is an example giving the dimensions of the detonator). This detonator is put together on the following way: 2 points of detonation with PTL in an explosive substance, a vibrating value making the PTL active, a fuse which goes through the detonator box to the trigger booster located in HE (highly explosive substance).

B. *Sphere of HE:*   the sphere is composed of 36 5-sided lenses. Each lens is composed of a series of parts;

     1.   HE (composition S) poured around a refractory substance.

     2.   the latter is composed of barium nitrate plus TNT. This is the medium which forces the shock waves to come into focus in such a way as to cause an implosion.

Abstract of David Greenglass report

ЗАМЕТКИ О КОНСТРУКЦИИ АТОМНОЙ БОМБЫ.

Описание конструкции бомбы типа "взрыва вовнутрь".

А. Детонатор: эта часть бомбы имеет два провода, подводящих к двум точкам детонации /Имеется образец, дающий размеры детонатора/. Этот детонатор составляется следующим образом: две точки детонации с РТХ в качестве взрывчатого вещества, вибрирующий клапан, приводящийся в действие РТХ, плавкий предохранитель, который проходит через ящик детонатора к ударнику бустера, находящегося в НЕ /сильно действующее взрывчатое вещество/.

В. Шар из НЕ: шар НЕ состоит из 36 пятиугольных линз. Каждая линза состоит из ряда частей;

1/ НЕ /состав С/, отлитое вокруг тугоплавкого вещества;

2/ последнее состоит из нитрата бария плюс ТNТ. Это и есть среда, которая заставляет ударные волны собираться в фокусе таким образом, чтобы вызвать взрыв вовнутрь.

in the United States had received material on the American atomic bomb project from Hall, Fuchs, Greenglass, and possibly other unknown individuals. With the exception of the Greenglass material, everything obtained had been sent to the Soviet Union with reasonable dispatch. But according to Albright and Kunstel, who based their conclusion on the various inventory records they had reviewed, the Greenglass report arrived three months after the other data. In the text of *Bombshell*, the authors wrote:

> . . . when NKGB chief Merkulov sent Beria the bomb design [of Hall and Fuchs] in all its intricate detail, Beria thought it looked too good to be true. Beria's doubts probably ballooned three months later, when Merkulov sent him another raw document that had been pouched from New York. Entitled "Notes on the Construction of the Atomic Bomb," it was a third version of how to design an implosion weapon. It was almost certainly the same muddled atomic bomb drawings that Sergeant Greenglass had passed to Julius Rosenberg during his September furlough in New York. Greenglass's design was not quite the same as the design Beria had approved, the one based on matching intelligence from Fuchs and from Lona Cohen's source in Albuquerque. One difference even Beria could grasp: The Greenglass version had "36 pentagonal lenses" in the outer layer of high explosives; Beria's approved bomb design had only thirty-two such lenses (p. 164).

But why, I wondered, had the Greenglass version of the bomb arrived in Moscow months after the data from Fuchs and others when all of this material was presumably gathered by Soviet intelligence at about the same time? Albright and Kunstel offer no reason for this three-month hiatus that their diligent probing had uncovered, and no other person that I was aware of had picked up on it either. Therefore when Miriam and I discussed all the unknowns, we agreed that until I had an explanation to offer, it would be prudent to keep word of my finding to ourselves and not write about or share it with anyone else.

But where to seek an explanation? It was public knowledge at the time that Allen Weinstein, a historian, had a book in progress based on information from KGB spy files. Moreover, I had recently been told by a reliable source that Weinstein had confided that the KGB data he had obtained for his book did include material on the Rosenberg case. Perhaps this forthcoming work might yield the answers I was seeking.

Meanwhile, the significance of the date December 27, 1945, remained an intriguing mystery.

TWO

Opening the KGB Archives

To suddenly and unexpectedly unearth new information about the Rosenberg affair was an exciting event, and it set my mind racing. I tried to rethink some of the material about David and Ruth Greenglass that I had gone over so many times before. When Miriam and I first studied the Rosenberg trial record, it was immediately evident to us that the principal prosecution witnesses were the Greenglasses. On that there was general agreement. The Court of Appeals for the Second Circuit had ruled: "Doubtless, if [the Greenglass] testimony were disregarded, the conviction could not stand." But it was also frustratingly evident to us then, as it was to me now, that the major accusations relating to atomic espionage that the Greenglasses had leveled against the Rosenbergs were essentially irrefutable. There was simply no evidence to prove or disprove their account. The Greenglasses told a story. The Rosenbergs denied the story. It was a classic he-said/she-said situation.

Naturally I couldn't resist a glimmer of hope that this old and seemingly insurmountable impasse might now at long last be resolved with the help of the fresh clues I had stumbled on—especially the enigmatic date December 27, 1945, relating to David Greenglass's report on the atomic bomb. I knew that the only major untapped source of material on the case was the Holy of Holies of the Cold War espionage universe: the KGB intelligence archives. That Allen Weinstein was then preparing a book based on those hitherto-sealed archives was a fantastic stroke of luck for me, and I impatiently awaited its publication.

I had to wait for more than a year.

• • •

Allen Weinstein is a historian who taught at Smith College and elsewhere. He is also a writer. His best-known book is *Perjury: The Hiss-Chambers Case* which, when it appeared in 1978, was widely acclaimed and catapulted him to national attention. It also precipitated a still-extant dispute between himself and then *Nation* editor Victor Navasky, whose request that he be permitted to check some of the book's documentation was denied by Weinstein. After about two decades in academia,

Weinstein made a major career change, moving into a far different and wider arena: international relations. In 1985, he founded and became president of the Center for Democracy, a small but surprisingly influential Washington-based organization that operated throughout the world with the stated goal of promoting and strengthening the democratic process. In this capacity he had contact with many top governmental leaders, both in Washington and abroad; the Center maintained an office in Moscow, and Weinstein is said to have been an advisor to Boris Yeltsin while the latter was president of Russia.

One of the interests of the Center was the role of intelligence organizations in a democratic state, and Weinstein has made no secret of the fact that he had intimate connections with the American intelligence community. For example, he has recounted that in 1993, several high-level Russian intelligence officials "visited the United States as my guests. Their meetings included a private talk with then-CIA Director R. James Woolsey at my home . . . and conversations with leading CIA and FBI counterintelligence officials at the request of those officials." In 1996, when a conference on the Venona decrypts was held at the National War College, it was jointly sponsored by the National Security Agency, the Central Intelligence Agency, and Weinstein's Center for Democracy.[5]

Allen Weinstein's new book, *The Haunted Wood: Soviet Espionage in America*, co-authored with a Russian, Alexander Vassiliev, finally appeared in early 1999.[6] Reviews were somewhat mixed. Thus the Sunday *New York Times* praised the book unreservedly, while the daily *Times* complained that "readers less familiar with the record will find much of the material fragmentary, convoluted, badly shaped, dryly written and, all in all, an exercise to make the eyes glaze over." Another reviewer, in the online magazine *Salon*, used words like "dull" and "boring" and said the book's organization "is haphazard and difficult to track. Names, dates, facts and figures are sprayed at the reader like a sneeze." Even an otherwise laudatory review in the *Journal of Cold War Studies* criticized the book's "minimal background" and "absence of context."

The moment I obtained a copy, I eagerly skipped straight to the pages on the atom spies, particularly the Greenglasses and Rosenbergs. Surprise after surprise unfolded. Far from dull and soporific, I found what I was reading mind-blowing, enthralling, incredibly exhilarating, and then, ultimately, infuriating and sad.

I reread the pages over and over, amazed that none of the reviewers had comprehended their import. Then gradually I understood why. Nowhere in the book had Weinstein (who appears to have been the primary author) alerted the reader to the fact that he and Vassiliev had made important discoveries about the Rosenberg case. Moreover, the book prints material from the KGB files on the Rosenbergs and Greenglasses but doesn't include relevant excerpts from the Rosenberg trial record, to enable the reader to compare the two versions. Such a comparison would have revealed that the authors had come up with new evidence that contradicts key prosecution testimony in the government's atom spy trial.

I have no idea why Weinstein hid his light under a bushel. But while I was perplexed at this unique shortcoming, it would be fair to say that I was also delighted, because it meant that I would have a crack at explicating Weinstein's and Vassiliev's remarkable but still unexamined findings.

But first I had the responsibility of any researcher working with material from an unfamiliar source: to learn as much as I could about its provenance and authenticity. The KGB documents utilized in the book are identified by their file, volume, and page numbers in the Russian intelligence archives. Ordinarily, this would be sufficient information to enable me to determine whether a quotation or fact in the book was copied or interpreted correctly simply by checking it against the original source. But I was dealing here with data from archives that are barred to the public. For all intents and purposes, the extensive source notes in the book refer the reader to an invisible archive. Performing due diligence on an invisible archive is definitely tricky.

From explanations provided by Allen Weinstein in *The Haunted Wood* and in various media interviews, I pieced together a partial picture of how and under what unusual conditions the KGB files were opened. The project had its beginnings a few years after the demise of the Soviet Union, a time that Weinstein describes as a "honeymoon period in Russian-American relations." More to the point, perhaps, it was also, for the Russians, a period of severe economic dislocation when the once-stable ruble plummeted in value, impoverishing those on fixed incomes, such as pensioners. The need for money was apparently the spur that led the Russians to divulge the contents of some of their closely guarded intelligence files. And, in fact, it was a group of retired KGB spooks, now fallen on hard times, who were in the forefront of the negotiations on the archives project.

According to Weinstein, in 1993, Alberto Vitale, then the president of Random House publishers, signed off on an agreement with this association of retired intelligence officers whereby the newly named Russian Foreign Intelligence Service (the SVR) would disclose information from old Soviet spy files of its predecessor agency, the KGB, to a number of Western scholars working on books with Russian co-authors. Many specifics of the deal have never been revealed, including who paid how much to whom; however, Weinstein assumes that the Russians received a "significant sum." Also unknown is why, of the four books eventually produced under this agreement—on the Cuban missile crisis, the Cambridge spies, the Berlin crisis, and Soviet espionage in America during the Stalin era—all but the last were issued by publishers other than Random House.[7]

The Russians set stringent guidelines for the project, imposing restrictions that violated customary practices for scholarly research. However, I hasten to add that most writers interested in the subject, myself included, would have accepted almost any conditions to have even secondhand access to KGB archives. Acting under those guidelines, Weinstein, sometime in 1994, visited the press and public affairs office of the SVR in downtown Moscow, where he was introduced to the co-author who had been picked for him, Alexander Vassiliev, a journalist and former KGB intelligence agent. Weinstein and Vassiliev were not permitted to work in the intelligence archives or even to visit the building where they were housed, which is located at the sprawling main Russian intelligence headquarters at Yasenevo outside Moscow. Instead, after they had prepared a plan for their book and provided the SVR with a copy, bound volumes of relevant documents were brought from the archives and delivered to Vassiliev at the press bureau. According to the agreed-upon ground rules, Weinstein was not allowed to see these raw files, which in any event were in Russian, in which he is not fluent.

Given the uniqueness of this arrangement, one might have expected that the book would include an essay that detailed the handling and provenance of its documentary sources, but instead Weinstein limited his comments on the subject to a few paragraphs:

> Our contract allowed Vassiliev, who had retired from the KGB in 1990 because of his opposition to Soviet leadership, to review archived documents and to make summaries or verbatim transcriptions from the files, including their record numbers. The documentary material, organized into topical areas, was then submitted to a panel of the SVR's leading officials for review and eventual release. Throughout this process, I worked alongside Vassiliev during more than two dozen visits to Moscow: monitoring the information found, prodding the SVR to expedite release of material submitted, and organizing Western primary and secondary research data essential to the book.
>
> As relations between the United States and Russia grew strained, the SVR became less cooperative

about providing timely release of the reviewed documentary materials. By late 1995, there were no more releases, and SVR officials had begun to express concern about the extensive and revealing data previously turned over. . . .

By that time we had received a critical mass of the released KGB material. Using Vassiliev's initial draft and translations while incorporating new Western documentation, I wrote the English-language manuscript, and Vassilev is now preparing *The Haunted Wood*'s Russian-language edition. The book was not submitted for SVR scrutiny before publication. . . .

In Moscow, meanwhile, a great deal of additional and important unreviewed KGB material reached us informally from other, non-KGB sources during our research and has been incorporated into the book. We thank those responsible for this help and have honored their requests for anonymity [pp. xv–xvii].

While helpful, this information was clearly incomplete, raising as many questions for me as it answered.[8] I wondered, for example, if the SVR officials withheld or censored any of the material Vassiliev submitted to them for release. Or if Vassiliev obtained any other archival material that he and Weinstein did not use, in whole or in part, in their book. As for the "great deal" of "important" KGB material that reached the authors "informally," were these actual KGB documents, summaries of them, or perhaps oral accounts; what cases did they deal with; and how, if at all, is this material cited in the book's sources?[9]

Also, the authors relegate to a footnote the fact that the KGB reports contain the code names of agents, not the real names. No doubt the real names often were obvious to the authors from the context, or became available later when the Venona decrypts were released. But were there instances where the authors relied largely on surmise?

I didn't anticipate any difficulty in obtaining answers from Allen Weinstein to these and other related questions. In 1996 after the Venona Conference in Washington, D.C., Weinstein had made friendly overtures to Miriam and me. He praised the piece on Venona and the Rosenberg case that we had written for *The Nation* and also our comments at the conference, and he urged us to visit him at his office the next time we were in the capital. We thanked him cordially, although, as it turned out, we were never able to accept his invitation. So when I communicated with him now, I was confident of a collegial response.

Inexplicably, Weinstein stonewalled. My letters, faxes, and e-mails went unanswered. My telephone calls were refused. Even my smallest requests for clarification were ignored.

Alternatively, I tried to get in touch with the book's co-author, Alexander Vassiliev. While working on *The Haunted Wood* in Moscow, Vassiliev had apparently done something that so displeased SVR officials that he decided to depart from Russia post-haste. In Weinstein's introduction to the book, he alluded to the matter circumspectly. At the end of a paragraph describing the "concern" of SVR officials who were having second thoughts about the extent of the information that he and Vassiliev had obtained, Weinstein added, without elaboration: "In 1996, Alexander Vassiliev accepted a journalist's assignment abroad and moved with his family to England." Elsewhere in the book, Vassiliev listed his whereabouts simply as "Western Europe." My attempts to locate and contact him proved futile. The promised Russian-language edition of the book he was said to be preparing has never been published.

• • •

Pursuing research that dead-ends is depressing, and I had about run out of ideas as to how I could verify the Weinstein-Vassiliev material. But then coincidence, even more capricious than usual, intervened to rescue my efforts. While working on our individual books, Miriam and I had been living for part of every year in San Miguel de Allende, a historic old city located 6,500 feet up in the mountains of central Mexico where a live-ly community of several thousand contented gringos (mainly Americans and Canadians) has taken root. It was to this most unlikely of places that two elderly witnesses to history, Mi-chael Straight and Zoya Zarubina, found their way, each with personal knowledge relating to the authenticity of the KGB material in *The Haunted Wood*.

The first arrival was Michael Straight. An entire chapter in *The Haunted Wood* is devoted to him, recounting how as a 20-year-old student at Cambridge University he was recruited by the KGB.

Michael Whitney Straight was an American blue-blood, a descendant on his mother's side of those ruthless financiers and industrialists who have come to be known as robber barons.

They were men who merged their families as purposefully as they did their companies. Grandmother Flora was a recipient of Standard Oil riches by way of her brother, Oliver Payne, a partner of John D. Rockefeller. Aunt Gertrude Vanderbilt Whitney was the great-granddaughter of Commodore Cornelius Vanderbilt, a tycoon who collected steamships and railroads. Michael's mother, Dorothy Payne Whitney, an heiress to the Whitney fortune, was a maverick who rejected her many millionaire suitors and, to the horror of her family and social set, chose neither hereditary wealth nor European nobility, marrying instead Willard Straight, a man who was merely a banker-diplomat associated with the powerful J.P. Morgan and Company. In 1914, the two founded a liberal magazine, *The New Republic*, and when Willard died in the devastating influenza pandemic that followed World War I, Dorothy maintained her ownership in the publication and her iconoclastic ways. Later, her son, Michael, while majoring in economics at Cambridge University, took a more radical path. Influenced by the Great Depression and rise of fascism, he joined the student communist movement and shared a bit of his family's fortune with the British Communist Party's newspaper, the *Daily Worker*.

In spring 1937, Michael, then in his senior year, vacationed in the United States. Seeking advice about his future career, he visited two old family friends at their home in Washington, D.C. Their home was called the White House, and the family friends were Franklin and Eleanor Roosevelt. After graduation, he worked for the New Deal, serving in the State

Department and later helping to write speeches for members of FDR's cabinet. Subsequently he joined the staff of *The New Republic*, and eventually became the magazine's editor.

A resilient octogenarian, Michael Straight had come to San Miguel to attend a board meeting of a local charity he supported and play a little tennis. He graciously agreed to be interviewed, and we met for drinks on the patio of his hotel, the Jacaranda, where the squawks of a caged macaw registered staccato interruptions on my tape recording.

I reminded him that he was probably the only remaining person who could evaluate the KGB archival material about him published by Weinstein and Vassiliev. Straight had no doubt that the authors had obtained his actual KGB intelligence file. Citing several statements and opinions and comments about himself in the KGB documents quoted in *The Haunted Wood*, he observed that they were "absolutely right—this is accurate all the way through." Similarly, he said that a detailed appraisal of his character from a KGB document reprinted in *The Haunted Wood* was "very accurate ... perfectly true." However, he felt that some documents describing his recruitment in England for the KGB (he had thought at the time that he was working for the Comintern) contained information about himself that, while otherwise factual, had been attributed to the wrong source—a Soviet agent he claimed never to have met. I asked Straight, did he think that mistakes might have been made by Vassiliev in copying his KGB file? "No, not at all," he responded.[10]

According to Straight's intelligence file, as reported in *The Haunted Wood*, after coming to the United States he met frequently with a KGB operative but never provided information of any value to the Soviets. Then, in 1939, he reacted with disappointment and sharp criticism to the signing of the Nazi-Soviet Pact, and afterward his contacts with KGB agents became infrequent, ending completely in 1942. In his interview with me, Straight confirmed that this account of his meetings in the United States reflected the actual events as he recalled them. In short, Straight was convinced that Vassiliev had seen his genuine KGB file and had transcribed the documents correctly.

Like Michael Straight, Zoya Zarubina is the sort of person to whom one speaks with an awed awareness that there is only one degree of separation between her and many major figures and events of the first half of the twentieth century. She is a Russian who comes from an extended family of KGB spies. Her father, Vassily Zarubin, served as the KGB's New York station chief during World War II. Her stepmother, Elizabeth Zarubina, an experienced KGB operative, also worked in the United States in the 1940s. Both are mentioned in *The Haunted Wood*, Vassily scores of times. Her stepfather (whom she called Uncle Leonid) was in his professional life the brutal KGB General Naum Eitingon, who arranged the assassination of Leon Trotsky in Mexico. And she herself was an intelligence agent and linguist from her early twenties, when she was assigned by the KGB to work at the Teheran conference, where she came into contact with Stalin, Roosevelt, and Churchill, as well as Molotov, Beria, and other leaders. She attended the summits at Yalta and Potsdam as an aide and interpreter and also the Nuremberg War Crimes Trials. In 1945–46 she translated technical material on the American atomic bomb that had been obtained by KGB foreign intelligence. Fluent in several languages, she subsequently had a career as a head interpreter for Soviet delegations at many international gatherings, including the years of meetings that led to the Helsinki Accords. She has served as Dean of the English Language Department at Moscow's Institute of Foreign Languages, taught at the Diplomatic Academy of the Ministry of Foreign Affairs, and directed the United Nations Language Training Center. She has also had a distinguished career in many peace and feminist women's organizations. Today, in Russia, she is a respected and well-connected person.

Zarubina had been invited to San Miguel de Allende to present a series of lectures on Russian history and to promote a recently published biography about herself. When I met her, I was carrying a copy of *The Haunted Wood*. Immediately, she informed me that she had read the book and turned to the index to show me the many references to her "parents." She also volunteered, with evident disapproval, that Vassiliev "ran off to England" and took some sort of research material with him, but when I pressed her about the incident, she refused to discuss it further. I then inquired if the documents quoted in the book had actually been obtained from the KGB archives; that is, were they "authentic"? Zoya Zarubina answered without hesitation: "Absolutely." Finally, I asked her if she believed that the information in the book from the KGB archives was true. She replied, with what I thought was considerable wisdom, "As much as possible."

• • •

The words of Straight and Zarubina bolstered my confidence in the authenticity of the KGB archival material in *The Haunted Wood*. And when I compared that material with Venona decrypts that mention the Rosenbergs and the Greenglasses, as well as Gold and Fuchs, I found the two sources consistent with each other. None of the decoded Venona messages on atomic espionage is at odds with the KGB files reported in the Weinstein book. In one instance, a puzzling Venona decrypt about Harry Gold has been clarified: It is apparently the reply to a message from Moscow now available from the KGB files. Venona and the KGB archives tell a similar story, but the former is far more fragmentary and therefore sometimes subject to misinterpretation. In effect, the KGB archives fill in the story told haltingly by Venona.

For the task ahead of me, I had on hand the Rosenberg trial record, the voluminous files secured through the Freedom of Information Act from the FBI and other federal agencies, and the Venona decrypts. But I also had an ace in the hole: the transmittal memo and abstract acquired by Albright and Kunstel from the Russian Ministry of Atomic Energy and sent to me by Michael Meeropol.

Thus armed, I opened the door to the KGB archives and found a whole new narrative of the Rosenberg case awaiting me.

THREE

A Pink Slip from Moscow

The name of Julius Rosenberg first appeared in the KGB archives in the early 1940s. A message from the KGB center in Moscow to its New York station mentioned in 1942 some political gossip that had been provided by "a stranger, Julius Rosenberg" and passed on by Jacob Golos, a veteran Soviet intelligence agent. That Rosenberg was a "stranger" to the KGB, despite the fact that he was already a source for Golos, was the result of Golos's peculiar modus operandi. A middle-aged man of Russian ancestry, Golos was well known in American Communist Party circles and was close to Earl Browder, head of the party. He managed two New York City companies—a travel agency and a parcel-shipping firm—both of which dealt entirely with the Soviet Union and had been set up covertly by the CP as business ventures. He was also an inveterate collector of a wide variety of information for the KGB, voraciously enlisting scores of American Communists and sympathizers as sources. He delivered this information to Soviet intelligence but refused to allow the KGB to formally recruit or even to know much, if anything, about his contacts. His contacts, in turn, were told that the information they were giving was intended for use by American Communist Party leaders, a fiction that some chose to believe while others, such as Julius Rosenberg, divined the real destination. At the time, Rosenberg was the leader of a CP cell consisting of four other engineers and was supplying data pilfered by himself and his comrades from their jobs in defense installations to Golos through a go-between, a CP functionary named Bernard Schuster.

Since technology was a terra incognita to Golos, his supervision of the output of this secret cell was haphazard. When a young KGB agent named Semyon Semyonov got an inkling of the situation, he checked the office files and determined that Golos's CP engineers were furnishing "desultory materials rated low in importance." However, Semyonov, who had recently earned a Master's degree in mechanical engineering at MIT and specialized in scientific and technical intelligence, believed that the group had "great potential possibilities." He appealed to his boss, station chief Vassily Zarubin (whose daughter, Zoya, I met so many years afterward in San Miguel de Allende), to transfer them to his control, and around late summer or early fall 1942 this was done, despite resistance by Golos. Semyonov, who recalled later that the 24-year-old Julius Rosenberg had been "absolutely unripe in matters of working as an agent," set himself the task of training him and the other raw recruits.

The decision of Semyonov's trainees to join this perilous enterprise may well have been influenced by the context of the times. Russia was engaged in a gargantuan struggle for survival against invading Nazi armies. In the United States, public sympathy for the Russian people was widespread. The American government was shipping vast quantities of Lend-Lease assistance to the Soviet Union, its wartime ally.

I can well imagine that the next two years were the most exciting and fulfilling of Julius Rosenberg's life. On a personal level, he and his wife Ethel, who had been living in his mother's apartment and in furnished rooms, had recently found their own three-room apartment in Knickerbocker Village in downtown Manhattan. And in March 1943, Ethel gave birth to a son, Michael. On a political level, Julius was a man with a head full of the fantasies about the Soviet Union then current among the far left, a blind faith in the goodness of a land he had never seen. Now, under Semyonov's tutelage, he was aiding that beleaguered land and, as he doubtlessly believed, thereby contributing to the defeat of fascism and the achievement of socialism throughout the world.

Julius Rosenberg was no great shakes as an engineer. His CCNY classmate and friend Morton Sobell always spoke to us of Julius's abilities as an engineer with gentle derision. According to Sobell, Julius had studied engineering merely because in those Depression years he couldn't think of any other field from which he might conceivably earn a living. As a youth, Julius had been deeply drawn to religion before encountering Marxism, and more than once Morty told us jokingly that Julius would have made a better rabbi than an engineer. But in his work for Soviet intelligence, he appears to have found his metier.

The Moscow KGB center praised his qualities as an organizer and recruiter and awarded bonuses to him and the other agents in his group. They admired his loyalty and devotion to the Soviet Union. According to a Venona decrypt, he had eight people working under his direction at the beginning of December 1944, after which the KGB—concerned that they might put him "out of action with overwork"—transferred some of his most productive agents out of his group to other supervisors. The real Julius Rosenberg depicted in the KGB archives and Venona was a far cry from the hapless leftist nonentity that Miriam and I and millions of others had pictured. He was an indefatigable Horatio Alger of spying who, from humble beginnings with Golos, zealously worked his way up to be a respected Soviet technical agent and group leader. Incredibly, he apparently continued his party connections, meeting monthly with his CP liaison, Bernard Schuster, and dutifully turning over to him party dues collected from the members of his group. Certainly only a few top Communist Party brass were aware of this arrangement, but their rashness in countenancing it is mind-boggling. Semyonov remained Rosenberg's controller until about spring 1944, when the Russian came under FBI surveillance and his protégé was transferred to another supervisor, Alexander Feklisov.

Life for most of us contains a few large what-ifs. One wonders: what if these two active years had been the full extent of Julius Rosenberg's espionage career? Were he alive today, an old man in a world more altered than he could ever have conceived, he might contemplate the actions of his youthful self with wry amusement, amazement, or possibly shame. Had he been caught, his punishment would have depended on the temper of the times. During World War II, when Russia was an ally, the affair might even have been hushed up as an embarrassment. During the Cold War, he would have faced a serious prison sentence. But however his involvement with KGB intelligence had played itself out, the endgame would not have involved a starring role in an international cause célèbre.

What made all the difference started with a letter from David Greenglass to his wife Ruth. It was in the summer of 1944. Out of the blue, David Greenglass was transferred from his overseas-bound military unit to the Manhattan Project and, after warnings about the need for tight security, he was sent to the secluded installation at Los Alamos, New Mexico, where he was assigned to duties as an Army machinist. His new address there was simply P.O. Box 1663, Santa Fe, New Mexico.

On the train en route to Los Alamos, he wrote a letter to Ruth:

Aug. 4, 1944 Dear, I have been very reticent in my writing about what I am doing or going to do because it is a classified top secrecy project and as such I can't say anything. In fact, I am not even supposed to say this much. Darling, in this type of work at my place of residence there is censorship of mail going out and all off the post calls. So dear, you know why I don't want you to say anything on the telephone. That is why I write C now dear instead of comrade. Your husband, lover and Comrade, Dave

P.S. . . . Not a word to anyone about anything except maybe Julie.

Obviously, Ruth did inform "Julie." But there is no indication that Julius Rosenberg reacted to the news of his brother-in-law's secret new job with any immediate interest. Perhaps his mind was on another, more mundane problem. For some months, Soviet intelligence in New York had been reorganizing the photographing of technical data, assigning various people, including Rosenberg, to the task and looking for secure places to do it. In September, Julius suggested to Feklisov that Ruth Greenglass's apartment could be used as a safe house for that purpose and provided details about her background and her husband's whereabouts.

A message sent from New York to Moscow on September 21, 1944, and later decrypted by the Venona project, said:

Lately the development of new people [has been in progress]. LIBERAL [Julius Rosenberg] recommended the wife of his wife's brother, Ruth GREEN-GLASS, with a safe flat in view. She is 21 years old, a TOWNSWOMAN [American], a GYMNAST [member of the Young Communist League] since 1942. She lives on STANTON Street. LIBERAL and his wife recommend her as an intelligent and clever girl. [undeciphered gap]

[Ruth] learned that her husband was called up by the army but he was not sent to the front. He is a mechanical engineer and is now working at the ENORMOZ [atomic bomb] plant in Santa Fe, New Mexico. [large undeciphered gap]

When the Russians heard where David was located, those agents responsible for ferreting out data on "Enormoz" apparently realized at once that he was employed on the atomic bomb project. The undeciphered gap in the Venona message can, in effect, be filled in by information now available in *The Haunted Wood* from the KGB archives. What Julius Rosenberg had had in mind when he mentioned Ruth and her apartment was a place where he and others could copy purloined documents. What the New York station was requesting, however, was permission to recruit both Greenglasses as agents. Moscow concurred on October 3, 1944, assigned a code name to David ("Bumblebee," later "Caliber") and one to Ruth ("Wasp"), and advised that they be handled directly by Harry Gold.[11] A later Venona decrypt reveals that New York demurred, noting that giving Gold, who was already handling Fuchs, so many of the atom bomb sources to deal with was "risky." New York proposed, instead, "To leave WASP and CALIBER in contact with LIBERAL until [undeciphered gap] work." What that "until" referred to remains unknown. By default, Julius became the Greenglasses' contact.

• • •

The charge in the Rosenberg trial was conspiracy to commit espionage; the defendants were all alleged to have been participants in a scheme aimed at obtaining national defense information for the benefit of the Soviet Union. That was certainly true of Julius. But the crux of the matter was the accusation that the Rosenbergs had stolen, with the aid of David Greenglass, the atomic bomb.

The trial that followed this awesome accusation lasted a mere fourteen days, unbelievably short by today's standards. But that part of the testimony comprising all of the government's evidence that incriminated Julius Rosenberg and Ethel Rosenberg in atomic espionage was far shorter still. A few hours of courtroom dialogue, nearly all by the Greenglasses, sent two people to their deaths.

The resemblance between trials and theater often has been remarked by lawyers. Skilled prosecutors have a touch of the playwright and organize evidence with an eye to its dramatic potential. The brief but lethal dialogue that doomed the Rosenbergs can readily be viewed as a three-act play.

Act one is the recruitment of the Greenglasses, a tale of how two innocents, Ruth and David, are ensnared into a terrible crime by their own relatives, the wily Julius and Ethel. The second act has two powerful and incriminating scenes: One concerns the passing of vital lens-mold sketches; the other, the cutting of a Jello box that will serve as a recognition device for a future spy rendezvous. Finally comes the climactic act three, in which Julius and Ethel's living room is the setting for the disclosure of the secret of the atomic bomb.

Act One. The Recruitment of the Greenglasses. The original story-line for act one was simple. It was first related by David Green-glass early in the morning of June 16, 1950—the day after he was picked up for questioning by the FBI—in a signed state-ment that began: "On or about November 29, 1944, my wife, Ruth, arrived in New Mexico from New York City and told me that Julius Rosenberg, my brother-in-law, had asked if I would give information on the Atom Bomb. . . ."

A month later, on July 17, after several days of interroga-tion by FBI agents and prosecutors, David signed a detailed confession in which he largely repeated his initial story of the recruitment. He said he had been solicited by Ruth, at the in-stance of Julius, and had immediately acquiesced. Recounting a conversation he had had with his wife while they were walk-ing along Route 66 in Albuquerque, where she visited him for their anniversary, David stated:

> . . . my wife Ruth told me that my brother-in-law, Julius Rosenberg, who is married to my sister Ethel, had asked Ruth to ask me to furnish information con-cerning the work I was doing at Los Alamos so that it could be furnished to the Soviet Government. . . . She said that my brother-in-law explained that we are at war with Germany and Japan and they are the enemy and that Soviet Russia is fighting the enemy and is therefore entitled to the information. Ruth told me that she did not like for me to get involved in this mat-ter as she thought it would cause trouble. I told Ruth,

however, that I would agree to give whatever information came to me in the course of my employment at
Los Alamos on the atom bomb project.

Ruth Greenglass also provided a confession on July 17, but in
her version of the recruitment, her sister-in-law Ethel emerged as
an important character who had been instrumental in persuading her to enlist David, and both she and David were portrayed
as unwilling participants. Whatever her thoughts and motives
were when she signed on to this account, she could scarcely have
dreamed that on that very day one of the most powerful men in
the United States, J. Edgar Hoover, would transmit her words to a
member of President Harry Truman's cabinet, Attorney General
J. Howard McGrath, and request him "to consider and advise us
whether there is sufficient evidence available on which to institute
prosecutive action against Ethel Rosenberg."

Also on that day, a top FBI official, Alan H. Belmont, hand-
delivered the memo to Assistant Attorney General James Mc-
Inerney, head of the Justice Department's Criminal Division.
Regarding the question of whether it was now possible to arrest
Ethel Rosenberg, Belmont reported that McInerney had replied
that there was "insufficient evidence to issue process against her
at this time. He advised that the evidence against her depends
upon the statement of Ruth Greenglass. . . . Mr. McInerney requested that any additional information concerning Ethel Rosenberg be furnished the Department. He was of the opinion that it
might be possible to utilize her as a lever against her husband."

Immediately, FBI agents revisited David in order to "rec-
oncile discrepancies" between his statement and Ruth's. Two

David Greenglass; Ruth Greenglass

David, Ruth, and Children; Ruth and Son

Julius Rosenberg, in custody of FBI agents following his arrest on July 17, 1950, as an "atom spy."

Ethel Rosenberg, interviewed by reporters in the kitchen of her apartment the day after her husband was jailed. A month later she was arrested.

Julius and Ethel Rosenberg during the trial.

Harry Gold (L) , arraigned in Philadelphia on May 23, 1950, as Fuchs' espionage accomplice. Klaus Fuchs (R), apprehended by British authorities on February 2, 1950, as a Soviet Agent.

Morton Sobell, at Newark Airport on August 23, 1950, en route from Laredo, Texas, to face espionage charges.

Shown left to right, *U.S. Attorney Irving Saypol and his assistants Myles Lane and Roy Cohn.*

Irving R. Kaufman, who, as a federal district judge, presided over the Rosenberg-Sobell trial.

David Greenglass at trial.

Ruth Greenglass at trial.

April 5, 1951. Ethel Rosenberg is escorted from the New York federal courthouse at Foley Square after being sentenced to die in the electric chair.

Death house visit. Defense attorney Emanuel Bloch at Sing Sing with the Rosenbergs' sons.

Execution Evening On June 19, 1953, Rosenberg sympathizers fill West Seventeenth Street in New York City.

David Greenglass, left, leaves prison in late 1960. At right, his attorney, O. John Rogge.

Walter Schneir (right) with Joel Barr. Charles Bridge, Prague, November 1990.

days after affixing his signature to a confession, David drastically altered his story of the recruitment by implicating his sister. He signed an addendum to his confession and, in language that parroted Ruth's statement, brought his account into conformity with hers. He now recalled that his sister Ethel had played an active role in persuading Ruth and himself and also that he had been a reluctant participant.

At the trial, David testified to this new version of the recruitment. He was questioned by prosecutor Roy Cohn:

> Q. Will you tell us, Mr. Greenglass, what your wife said and what you said?
>
> A. . . . . Ethel started the conversation by stating to Ruth that she must have noticed that she, Ethel, was no longer involved in Communist Party activities. . . . And he [Julius] then went on to tell Ruth that I was working on the atomic bomb project at Los Alamos and that they would want me to give information to the Russians. My wife objected to this, but Ethel said. . . .
>
> The Court: Did your wife use the word "object"?
>
> A. She told me that she didn't think it was a good idea. . . . And that she didn't want to tell me about it. . . . But they told her that I would want to know about it and I would want to help, and that at least—the least she could do was tell me about it. So that was the conversation. At first—she asked me what I thought about that—at first, I was frightened and worried about it and I told her. . . . that

I wouldn't do it. And she had also told me that in the conversation, Julius and Ethel had told her that Russia was an ally and as such deserved this information, and that she wasn't getting the information that was coming to her. So later on that night after this conversation, I thought about it and the following morning I told my wife that I would give the information.

When Ruth's turn came to testify, she told a similar story about the recruitment, stressing both her reluctance to take part and Ethel's alleged insistence that she do so. Ruth recounted for the jury her November 1944 conversation with Julius Rosenberg:

> . . . . He said he wanted me to tell my husband David that he should give information to Julius to be passed on to the Russians. And, at first I objected to this. I didn't think it was right. I said that the people who are in charge of the work on the bomb were in a better position to know whether the information should be shared or not.
>
> Ethel Rosenberg said that I should at least tell it to David, that she felt that this was right for David, that he would want it, that I should give him the message and let him decide for himself, and by the— Julius and Ethel persuaded me to give my husband the message. . . .

Testifying about her later conversation with her husband in Albuquerque, Ruth again emphasized the role of Ethel:

> . . . . [I] told him that I had objected to it but that Ethel had told me that David would be interested, that he would want this, that this was right for him, and that I should at least tell him about it, and my husband did not give me an immediate answer; at first he, too, refused, and the following day he told me that he would consent to do this.

Of course, neither the jurors nor the defense had any idea at the time of the trial that David's testimony implicating his sister in his recruitment contradicted his earlier confessions. Those confessions were not publicly available until decades after the executions, when they were pried from the FBI by long litigation under the Freedom of Information Act.

Also obtained through the Freedom of Information Act was an unanticipated and fascinating find—the Greenglass wartime correspondence, a large number of handwritten letters exchanged by David and Ruth and seized by FBI agents from an old footlocker in their apartment on the day David was taken into custody. The importance of the letters is that they disclose something of the Greenglasses' actual state of mind, as opposed to the personas they presented to the jurors. In their courtroom testimony, the Greenglasses cast themselves as an extraordinarily malleable couple with no apparent reason for their misdeeds other than the influence of the Rosenbergs. The prosecution followed this line, and U.S. Attorney Saypol excoriated Julius and Ethel for "dragging" David into the conspiracy.

All of the letters below were written in 1943 and 1944, prior to the recruitment. In their private communications, the two frequently discussed their political convictions. Like the early apostolic Christians who had abiding faith that the Last Judgment was imminent and would occur in their own lifetimes, David and Ruth were convinced that a socialist world was almost within their grasp. David wrote to Ruth:

> Dearest, I love you because we have such similar ideals and beliefs. These beliefs are the cement with which our physical and emotional affection is welded into what humanity calls love.

As for the "ideals and beliefs" that David was referring to, day after day he expressed them in his intimate letters to his wife:

> In the end it will be Europe and a large part of Asia that will turn Socialist and the American end [of] the world will of necessity follow in the same course. So, dear, we still look forward to a Socialist America. And we shall have that world in our life time.

• • •

> Of late I have been having the most wonderful discussions on our native American fascists and I have

been convincing the fellows right along. I'll have my company raise the Red flag yet.

. . .

I love you with all the love of Marx and the humanity of Lenin.

. . .

Darling, I have been reading a lot of books on the Soviet Union. Dear I can see how farsighted and intelligent those leaders are. They are really geniuses every one of them. I have been revising what I think and how I think politically. Having found out all the truth about the Soviets, both good and bad I have come to a stronger and more resolute faith and belief in the principles of Socialism and Communism. I believe that every time the Soviet Government used force they did so with pain in their hearts and the belief that what they were doing was to produce good for the greatest number. The tremendous sacrifices of blood sweat and tears of the Soviet peoples is a feat that surpasses all sacrifices of the past. More power to the Soviet Union and a fruitful and abundant life for their peoples.

As for Ruth Greenglass, her political creed was just as starry-eyed and apocalyptic as her husband's. Here she wrote to him after a May Day rally:

Well sweetheart all I can say is that I am sorry I missed so many other May Days when I had the opportunity to march side by side with you. . . . Perhaps the voice of 75,000 working men and women that were brought together today—perhaps their voice demanding an early invasion of Europe will be heard and then my dear we will be together to build—under socialism—our future.

Other letters of Ruth's expressed similar sentiments:

Still darling I hope that our children will be brought up in a socialist world and our money will be useless, I look forward to that day when necessities and luxuries are to be had by all and sundry just so long as he justifies living by working.

For me, reading these letters provided the first hint of a different scenario, one in which the Greenglasses' part in the drama might have been more complex than that of passive dupes. What if from the start they were willing actors in the plot? Not just compliant tools of Julius, but people motivated by dreams and beliefs of their own?

Another hint came years later, with the release of the decoded Venona messages. In one, David was described as having "given thought" to providing information for the Russians even before he was recruited by Ruth. It was sent from New York to Moscow on December 16, 1944.

WASP [Ruth Greenglass] has returned from a trip to see CALIBER [David Greenglass]. CALI-BER expressed his readiness to help in throwing light on the work being carried on at Camp-2 [Los Alamos] and stated that he had already given thought to this question earlier. CALIBER said that the authorities of the Camp were openly taking all precautionary measures to prevent information about ENORMOZ falling into Russian hands. This is causing serious discontent among the progressive [workers]. . . .

In researching the KGB archives, Alexander Vassiliev came upon what he and Allen Weinstein aptly call a "remarkable" document. The KGB's standard operating procedure was for agents to write up detailed descriptions of their meetings. After the recruitment meeting with Ruth, Julius diligently filed such a report. This is the kind of material that historians cherish: a contemporaneous document prepared in the ordinary course of business. In it, Ruth's language as quoted by Julius echoes the political rhetoric in the letters extolling socialism and the Soviet Union that she and her husband exchanged during the same period.

Julius's account of the discussion, which he related in the third person, said:

The following is a record of the conversation held by Julius, Ethel, and Ruth.

First of all, Julius inquired of Ruth how she felt about the Soviet Union and how deep in general her Communist convictions went, whereupon she replied without hesitation that, to her, socialism was the sole hope of the world and the Soviet Union commanded her deepest admiration.

Julius then wanted to know whether she would be willing to help the Soviet Union. She replied very simply and sincerely that it would be a privilege; when Ethel mentioned David, she assured us that [in] her judgment [this] was also David's understanding.

Julius then explained his connections with certain people interested in supplying the Soviet Union with urgently needed technical information it could not obtain through the regular channels and impressed upon her the tremendous importance of the project on which David is now at work. Therefore, she was to ask him the following kinds of questions:

1. How many people were now employed there?
2. What part of the project was already in operation, if any; were they encountering any difficulties and why; how were they resolving their problems?
3. How much of an area did the present setup cover?
4. How many buildings were there and their layout; were they going to build any more?
5. How well guarded was the place?

Julius then instructed her that under no circumstances should they discuss any of these things inside a room or indeed anywhere except out-of-doors and under no circumstances to make any notes of any kind. She was simply to commit to memory as much as possible. Ethel here interposed to stress the need for the utmost care and caution in informing David of the work in which Julius was engaged and that, for his own safety, all other political activity and discussion on his part should be subdued.

Other than the reference to Ethel having "mentioned David," her only contribution to the conversation related in the report was to express concern for the safety of her husband and her brother.[12] A Venona decrypt of a message sent to Moscow by the Soviet intelligence station in New York, summarizing Julius's account of the recruiting conversation, did not even allude to Ethel. The message noted that "[Julius Rosenberg] held a conversation with [Ruth Greenglass] about her assistance to us" and she had "expressed confidence that [David Greenglass] would agree to help."

For what it may be worth, we also have David Greenglass's own repudiation of his trial testimony about the recruitment.

Sam Roberts, a veteran *New York Times* journalist, tape-recorded fifty hours of interviews with David for a biography, published in 2001, with the omnibus title, *The Brother: The Untold Story of Atomic Spy David Greenglass and How He Sent His Sister, Ethel Rosenberg, to the Electric Chair.*[13] Roberts wrote: "David also testified that when Ruth first broached the Rosenbergs' invitation to commit espionage, he was frightened and didn't sign on as a spy until the following morning. Again, he was falsely portraying himself. . . ."

Roberts reported that when he questioned David about

his reaction to Ruth's message about furnishing information, David revealed: "The testimony at the trial is not what I actually felt at that time. I wasn't at all frightened by that. I never even thought twice about it. I was indoctrinated. I was ready for this."

Then Roberts asked David whether, when Ruth had recruited him, she was "quoting Ethel or Julius?"

Disregarding the account which he had told the jurors at the trial, David replied: "She was quoting Julius" [pp. 477–78].

• • •

Act Two, Scene One. The Lens Mold Sketches. In the Los Alamos shop where he worked, David Greenglass machined apparatus requested by scientists, including various kinds of molds used to cast high explosives into special shapes called lenses. On January 1, 1945, a month after his recruitment, he returned to New York City for several weeks on furlough. At the trial, he testified that while home he had drawn and turned over to Julius Rosenberg sketches of lens molds, along with accompanying explanatory information. A sketch that he had made for the trial was introduced as a replica of one he had passed.

Once again, the jurors and defense were unaware of the process by which David's story of the lens mold sketches had come into being. In the confession he signed on July 17, 1950, David said nothing about sketches. He stated that during his January furlough he had given Rosenberg a list of names of potential espionage recruits. He also recalled a brief car ride with an unknown man to whom Julius had introduced him, who asked questions about "a high-explosive lens" that David was unable to answer. The passing of such nondescript information by David could hardly have fulfilled the requirements of the prosecution.

Over two weeks later, while being prepped for a grand jury appearance, David was interrogated by Myles J. Lane, chief assistant U.S. Attorney:

> Q. At any time during the furlough did you make any sketches?
>
> A. I think I made a couple of lens [sic].
>
> Q. And he [Rosenberg] took them, didn't he?
>
> A. Yes, I suppose he did. . . .
>
> Q. In New York City did you give him sketches?
>
> A. Yes.
>
> Q. Whereabouts.
>
> A. I don't remember.
>
> Q. At your home?
>
> A. At my home.
>
> Q. Stanton Street?
>
> A. 266 Stanton Street.
>
> Q. Was he after you all the time, dunning you to give him more information?
>
> A. Oh, yes, trying to get me to give information; actually I didn't have too much information and then again I was on furlough.

However, by the time of the trial, David's enlarged story had been spruced up considerably. He testified that several days after he arrived home, Julius Rosenberg came to his apartment and asked him "for anything of value on the atomic bomb." Roy Cohn questioned him:

Q. Will you tell us just what information you furnished him with on that day?

A. . . . . I gave him some sketches of flat type lens molds, and I gave him some possible recruits . . . for espionage. . . .

Q. Tell us exactly what you gave Rosenberg with reference to the lens mold?

A. I gave him a sketch of the lens mold. I marked them, A, B, C, the parts of the mold, and I defined what these markings meant. . . . On a separate sheet of paper.

Cohn then drew Ethel into the action:

Q. By the way, did you have any conversation with Rosenberg concerning the writing on the descriptive material?

A. I did. My wife . . . in passing remarked that the handwriting would be bad and would need interpretation, and Julius said there was nothing to worry about as Ethel would type it up, retype the information.

Later, Ruth Greenglass repeated the same formulation, about David's poor penmanship necessitating the typing by Ethel of his handwritten material. She also added a conversation with Ethel:

> Well, Ethel said that she was tired and I asked her what she had been doing. She said she had been typing; and I asked her if she had found David's notes hard to distinguish. She said no, she was used to his handwriting.

In his summation, Irving Saypol reminded the jurors of Ethel's participation:

> He [David] came to New York on a furlough in January, 1945. It was on that furlough that Rosenberg received the first sketches of a high explosive lens. It was on that furlough that the descriptive material was given to Mrs. Rosenberg to be typed up.

Neither of the Greenglasses had said a word about Ethel typing in their confessions (nor did Ruth in her grand jury testimony).[14] It was Ruth, questioned by the FBI and prosecution only ten days before the trial, who first came up with the tale. Just before "opening night," Ethel's bit part was expanded. Mata Hari, it seems, had been a typist. Two days later, David followed his customary practice and confirmed his wife's last-minute account.

In 1979, in the only interview about the case she has ever given, Ruth Greenglass remarked: "At a certain point the agents became friends . . . they can elicit whatever they want from you."

I cannot resist wondering what might have been had Ethel's legal defense acted more resourcefully and aggressively on her behalf. Emanuel Bloch, the Rosenberg's attorney, was aware that in previous cases, left-wing attorneys like himself who had doggedly defended Communists had been punished afterward by being jailed for contempt of court and disbarred. Nominally, Ethel had an attorney of her own, Bloch's father, but he was of little help; his specialty was commercial real estate and he had no experience in criminal law. During the trial both men often behaved in a deferential, even obsequious, manner; possibly they believed this would benefit their clients, who were being tried in the midst of the Korean War. Perhaps the sexism of the period was also a factor. Whatever the reasons, the vulnerabilities of the prosecution's case against Ethel never were probed. David's letters demonstrate that his handwriting was by no means illegible, but the defense failed to introduce any evidence about this.

Now at long last intelligence documents have surfaced that divulge the data David Greenglass actually supplied to Julius in January 1945. What they show is that during his furlough David did not provide the Russians with any lens mold sketches. The damaging testimony about the lens sketches—including of course the testimony about Ethel typing the "descriptive material"—was a lie. The proof is in two Venona decrypts and a longer report secured by Weinstein and Vassiliev from the KGB archives.

The December 16, 1944, Venona document from the New York KGB office to the Moscow center disclosed:

> [In] the middle of January CALIBER [David Greenglass] will be in TYRE [New York City]. LIBERAL, referring to his ignorance of the [atomic energy] problem, expresses the wish that our man should meet CALIBER and interrogate him personally. He asserts that CALIBER would be very glad of such a meeting. Do you consider such a meeting advisable? If not, I shall be obliged to draw up a questionnaire and pass it to LIBERAL. Report whether you have any questions of priority interest to us.

As it turned out, the Russians did both. They drew up a list of questions for Julius to ask David and also apparently had one of their people meet with him personally in a car David was driving. A Venona message from New York to Moscow on January 8, 1945, read:

> CALIBER has arrived in TYRE [New York City] on leave. He has confirmed his agreement to help us. In addition to the information passed to us through WASP [Ruth Greenglass] he has given us a hand-written plan of the lay-out of Camp-2 and facts known to him about the work and the personnel. The basic task of the camp is to make the mechanism which is to serve as the detonator. Experimental work is being

carried out on the construction of a tube of this kind and experiments are being tried with explosive [undeciphered gap].

Finally, a fuller report on the information passed by David during his January furlough was obtained from the KGB archives. Again, it contained no reference to any sketches. As cited in *The Haunted Wood*, the report sent from New York to Moscow read:

[Julius Rosenberg] and [David Greenglass] met at the flat of [Greenglass's] mother . . . [Rosenberg's] wife and [Greenglass] are sister and brother. . . . [Rosenberg] discussed with him a list of questions to which it would be helpful to have answers . . . general questions clarifying the kind of work done there.

. . . . The place where [Greenglass] works is a plant where various devices for measuring and studying the explosive power of various explosives in different forms (lenses) are being produced. Experimental explosions are being carried out in proving grounds. . . . As far as we understand, research and selection of explosives for imparting a necessary speed to "ENORMOZ's" neutrons to get fission (explosion) are being executed in those proving grounds. It seems to us that [Greenglass] doesn't know all the details of the project. At the end of his report he lists people whom he considers progressive and pro-Soviet.

The irony is that it would not have made a whit of difference to the Russians had David really given Julius any of his sketches of experimental lens molds during that January furlough. David's sketches were rough; his knowledge of the design and composition of the explosive lenses was rudimentary to nonexistent. But at the trial, as a result of deft questioning of the government's expert witness by the prosecution and judge, the jurors may have been gulled into believing that David's crude drawings were matters of vast import.

Some months after the January furlough, on June 3, 1945, David apparently did pass sketches of lens mold experiments—not to Julius in New York City but to Harry Gold in Albuquerque. Gold was the only witness to attest to the great significance that the Russians ascribed to the sketches. He related to the jury what happened after he delivered the material from David Greenglass, along with material from Klaus Fuchs, to Anatoli Yakovlev/Yatskov. The performance was vintage Harry Gold:

> . . . . Yakovlev told me that the information that I had given him some two weeks previous had been sent immediately to the Soviet Union. He said that the information that I had received from Greenglass was extremely excellent and very valuable.

But a document found by Vassiliev in the KGB archives confirms what Miriam and I had long suspected: that this damning testimony by Harry Gold was a fabrication. The KGB, far from appraising the Greenglass material as "extremely excellent and very valuable," regarded it as of negligible worth, as indicated by Vassiliev's record of a cable sent by New York to the Moscow center:

> [Greenglass's] material, though it gives some data, is low in quality and far from processed. We suppose this is due to the insufficient qualifications of [Greenglass], on the one hand, and to [Gold's] sudden arrival, on the other, when he had no prepared materials.[15]

Act Two, Scene Two. The Jello Box. First mention of the cut Jello box, the best-known recognition device in the literature of espionage, occurred in the statement David signed on June 16, 1950, the day of his arrest, when he said he had identified Harry Gold by means of "a torn or cut piece of card."

> I cannot recall at this time whether this torn piece of card was given to me by my wife, Ruth, at the time she moved to Albuquerque, New Mexico, from New York about February, 1945, or whether I received it from Julius Rosenberg while I was in New York City on furlough. . . .

In his July 17 confession, David said he still could not remember whether the "torn piece of cardboard" had been given to him in Albuquerque by his wife or in New York by Julius. Ruth's confession took an entirely different tack. It was she who identified the card as a part of a Jello box and who said that it had been cut at the Rosenberg apartment one evening in early January while she and David were dinner guests there. She said Julius had cut the box in the presence of Ethel, David, and herself and had given one half to David.

David thereupon adopted Ruth's account of the Jello box episode in the Rosenberg apartment, discarding his earlier suggestion that his first knowledge of the "torn piece of card" had occurred when Ruth brought it with her to Albuquerque in late February.

For reasons unknown, a few weeks later both the Greenglasses amended their stories, insisting that David had not witnessed the cutting of the Jello box, nor seen the cut piece until Ruth showed it to him later at their New York apartment; this also was the narrative which Ruth recounted in her grand jury testimony. And at the trial, the cutting scene underwent yet another permutation. Though David was not present in the kitchen, he did assert that he had been shown the cut box immediately afterward. He presented this nicely polished final version in the courtroom:

Well, Rosenberg and my wife and Ethel went into the kitchen and I was in the living room; and then a little while later, after they had been there about five minutes or so, they came out and my wife had in her hand a Jello box side. . . . And it had been cut, and Julius had the other part to it, and when he came in with it, I said, "Oh, that is very clever," because I noticed how it fit, and he said, "The simplest things are the cleverest."

Both the Greenglasses testified that during the evening details had been discussed for a future pickup of information from David by a courier, who would be identified by the matching piece of the Jello box. With this testimony, the Jello box (together with the Julius password) became what prosecutor Saypol called a "necessary link" that connected the Rosenbergs to the later meeting of Harry Gold with the Greenglasses in Albuquerque. Ruth Greenglass, sounding in the words of writer Sam Roberts "downright biblical," related that when Julius gave her the cut portion of the box he said:

> This half will be brought to you by another party and he will bear the greetings from me and you will know that I have sent him.

By then, the January furlough and particularly the dinner at the Rosenberg apartment had grown into a significant part of the government's atom spy case. For Ethel, the Jello box scene was one more nail in her coffin.

But now a KGB report as transcribed by Vassiliev puts the Jello box affair in a startling new perspective. When I first read the report, its full meaning evaded me; then I did a double-take. I read it over four or five times until I fully absorbed its implications. They took my breath away. For the message invalidates David and Ruth's entire testimony about the Jello box episode.

It is a communication from the New York KGB station to the Moscow center, dispatched on February 17, 1945.[16]

This was over a month after Ruth had supposedly received a Jello box piece in the Rosenberg kitchen and long after David's furlough had ended and he had returned to Los Alamos. But the KGB document reveals that at this late date the recognition device, or "material password" in the lexicon of Soviet intelligence, had not yet even been chosen. Moreover, the person charged by the KGB with the task of choosing it was not Julius, but none other than Ruth herself. In fact, the message makes clear that Ruth was viewed by the KGB as a full-fledged agent in her own right, ready and willing to carry out assigned missions as a courier. The message reads:

> In late February, as soon as she receives a railroad ticket, [Ruth Greenglass] will go to live in Albuquerque, where most wives of camp workers live. . . . She intends to live there for 6–7 months and then return to [New York] to give birth to a child. Before her departure, we will ask her to give us material and verbal passwords in case we need to restore contact with her. After . . . finding an apartment, she will give us her address in a letter to her mother-in-law. We assume that [Ruth's] stay in Albuquerque will allow us to study better the working procedures and people at the camp and, in case [David] has valuable data, she can come to [New York] to inform us.

That Ruth was to provide a recognition device before she departed for New Mexico in late February dovetails with

David's jettisoned early confession, in which he said he may have been given the "torn or cut piece of card" by his wife after she had moved to Albuquerque. Based on the KGB report, it seems a fair surmise that Ruth herself—in her own New York City apartment on Stanton Street—selected a part of a Jello box for a recognition device, cut it in half, and retained one piece. By whatever route the other piece reached the Russians, one thing is clear: the famous Jello box scene in the Rosenbergs' apartment was strictly a product of Ruth Greenglass's imagination. The only prosecution evidence connecting the Rosenbergs to the Gold-Greenglass Albuquerque meeting was the "Julius" password—which has long been discredited[17]—and the Jello box. Absent the Jello box scene in the Rosenberg kitchen, that connection, so central to the prosecution case, is severed completely. Thus the KGB report on Ruth effectively demolishes the damaging charge by U.S. Attorney Irving Saypol in his summation that Julius Rosenberg had "arranged" the June 1945 atomic espionage rendezvous in New Mexico.

The analogy between a trial and a play had served me well for the first two "acts," but then I was abruptly stymied by a wholly unexpected piece of KGB material that did not fit at all into the plot of the case. Put succinctly, what transpired at this point in the story was that Julius Rosenberg received a pink slip from Moscow. Politely but firmly, the KGB laid him off, relieving him of his duties as a spy.

This incredible turn was a response by the KGB center to the news that Julius had been fired from his government job. His dismissal was mentioned briefly at the trial, and more details became available years later with the release of formerly secret Army and FBI files. They showed that on February 10, 1945, Julius Rosenberg had been suddenly cashiered by the Army from his position as a Signal Corps inspector on a charge of Communist Party membership. The FBI had burglarized Communist Party offices some months previously, in an illegal operation called a black-bag job, and photographed membership records. However, what was never considered by any students of the case was the response of Soviet intelligence when they learned that their very active agent Julius had been discharged. The KGB archives provide the answer.

The KGB regarded the firing of Julius as a potential security crisis that threatened to unravel their network. It was an alarm bell, and they reacted quickly. On February 16, 1945, a memorandum from Moscow to New York listed the measures to be taken. Weinstein described the contents of the message in *The Haunted Wood*: "It ordered Rosenberg released from his duties as a group handler, directed that all his sources (including the Greenglasses, presumably) be transferred to other controllers, and instructed Alexander Feklissov to stop meeting Rosenberg. This cable also ordered future contact between Julius and Feklissov to be made through a courier. Moscow recommended Lona Cohen."

A week later, on Febrary 23, 1945, Moscow sent a message to Leonid Kvasnikov, the KGB's scientific-technical chief in New York. As presented in *The Haunted Wood*, it said:

The latest events with [Julius Rosenberg], his having been fired, are highly serious and demand on our part, first, a correct assessment of what happened, and second, a decision about [Rosenberg's] role in future. Deciding the latter, we should proceed from the fact that, in him, we have a man devoted to us, whom we can trust completely, a man who by his practical activities for several years has shown how strong is his desire to help our country. Besides, in [Rosenberg] we have a capable agent who knows how to work with people and has solid experience in recruiting new agents.

One must suppose that, besides the motive stated when sacking [Rosenberg] of his belonging to the compatriots [the CP], the competitors [the FBI] may have other data compromising him, including information on his liaison with us. Proceeding precisely from this, we think that [Rosenberg] shouldn't start any legal actions to restore his job, leaving this matter to the trade-union, which must do what is being done for other members of the trade-union in this sort of case. There shouldn't be pressure from [Rosenberg] on this matter.

Though we don't have any documentary data, saying that the [FBI is] aware to an extent of his connection with us, we, nevertheless, must take into account the circumstances preceding [Rosenberg's] sacking—his extremely active work, especially in the first period working with us, and his certain haste in the work. We consider it necessary to take immediate measures to secure both [Rosenberg] and the agents with whom he was connected.

Before ceasing direct connection with [Rosenberg], it is necessary to explain to him the need to halt personal contact and to instruct him about the need to be careful, to look around himself. One should continue paying him maintenance. Warn him not to take any important decisions about his future work without our knowledge and consent. In our current relations with him, it must be explained that his fate is far from indifferent to us, that we value him as a worker, and that he, undoubtedly, may and must rely on assistance from our side.

Neither of the two KGB messages said a word about Ethel.

As for Julius, his career as a group handler for Soviet intelligence was over. So too was his regular relationship with Feklisov, who only rarely met with Julius again before leaving the United States in fall 1946.

• • •

The more I contemplated the KGB documents disclosing how in early 1945 Julius had been removed from his intelligence activities, the more I realized with what astounding consequence these documents were freighted. For the directives they convey are incompatible with Act Three of the courtroom drama, the September 1945 meeting in the Rosenberg apartment where the secret of the atom bomb changes hands—a meeting that is the capstone of the government's atom spy case. To say I was rocked back on my heels is an understatement.

FOUR

A Smoking Gun?

Act Three. The Secret of the Atomic Bomb. When David Greenglass related on the witness stand how in September 1945 he and Ruth had paid a momentous visit to the home of Julius and Ethel Rosenberg, carrying with them what Judge Kaufman later termed "the atom bomb secret," his account was front-page news throughout the United States.

The *New York Times* headlined its story "Atom Bomb Secret Described in Court," and observed:

On the stand, Greenglass wove a verbal net that encompassed his wife, Ruth, his sister, Ethel Greenglass Rosenberg, and her husband Julius Rosenberg.

The day before, prosecutor Roy Cohn had put David through his paces, questioning him about what had occurred during his September furlough to New York. David testified that Julius had come up to the apartment where he and Ruth were staying.

> Q. What did he say to you?
> A. He said to me that he wanted to know what I had for him. . . . I told him "I think I have a pretty good . . . description of the atom bomb."
> Q. The atom bomb itself?
> A. That's right. . . .
> Q. What did he say to you at that point?
> A. He said he would like to have it immediately, as soon as I possibly could get it written up he would like to get it. . . . during this conversation, he gave me two hundred dollars and he told me to come over to his house.

David interjected that Ruth had been opposed to giving any further information, but he had overruled her.

> Q. Did you draw up a sketch of the atom bomb itself?
> A. I did.
> Q. Did you prepare descriptive material to explain the sketch of the atom bomb?
> A. I did.
> Q. Was there any other material that you wrote up on that occasion?

A. I gave some scientists' names, and I also gave some possible recruits for espionage.

Q. Now about how many pages would you say it took to write down all of these matters?

A. I would say about twelve pages or so.

Q. . . . . Now tell us what you did after you prepared these twelve pages of written material, including the sketch of the atom bomb and a description of the sketch.

A. My wife and myself . . . drove around to Julius's house. We went up to the house and I gave Julius the information. . . .

Q. By the way, who was present when you handed the written material including this sketch over to Rosenberg?

A. My wife, my sister, Julius, and myself.

Q. By your sister, you mean Mrs. Rosenberg?

A. That is right.

Q. Now, will you tell us just what happened, Mr. Greenglass, after you handed this sketch and the descriptive material concerning the atomic bomb to Rosenberg? . . .

A. Well, he stepped into another room and he read it and he came out and he said "This is very good. We ought to have this typed up immediately." And my wife said, "We will probably have to correct the grammar involved," because I was more interested in writing down the technical phrases of it than I was in correcting the grammar. So they pulled—they had a bridge table and they brought it into the living room, plus a typewriter.

Q. What kind of typewriter?

A. A portable.

Q. Then what?

A. And they set that up and each sentence was read over and typed down in correct grammatical fashion.

Q. Who did the typing, Mr. Greenglass?

A. Ethel did the typing and Ruth and Julius and Ethel did the correction of the grammar.

Immediately after David left the witness stand, prosecutor James Kilsheimer questioned Ruth:

Q. Now what occurred in the Rosenbergs' apartment on that afternoon in September of 1945?

A. David gave Julius the written information. Julius said he was very pleased to get it and he went into another room to read it over, and after he read it he said this had to be gotten out immediately and he wanted Ethel to type it right away. . . and Ethel got out a typewriter and sat down to work on the notes.

Q. On what type of typewriter was it? I mean, was it a standard model or a portable model or what?

A. It was a portable—I believe it was a Remington.

Q. And where was the typewriter placed?

A. On the bridge table.

Q. All right. Now what occurred after the type-writer was placed on the bridge table?

A. Well, Ethel was typing the notes and David was helping her when she couldn't make out his hand-writing and explained the technical terms and spelled them out for her, and Julius and I helped her with the phraseology when it got a little too lengthy, wordy.

That was it—all of the government's evidence directly in-criminating the Rosenbergs in the paramount episode of The Great Atom Spy Robbery. Even now, rereading the trial re-cord, I could scarcely believe that this was the total testimony linking Julius and Ethel to what Roy Cohn called "the atom bomb itself." With these banal interchanges about a bridge table, a portable typewriter, and grammatical parsing, Ethel's death warrant was sealed. Summing up to the jurors, chief prosecutor Irving Saypol charged:

> On David's September furlough Rosenberg got from him the cross-section sketch of the atom bomb itself and a twelve-page description of this vital weapon. This description of the atom bomb, destined for deliv-ery to the Soviet Union, was typed up by the defendant Ethel Rosenberg that afternoon at her apartment at 10 Monroe Street. Just so had she on countless other oc-casions sat at that typewriter and struck the keys, blow by blow, against her own country in the interests of the Soviets.

Almost thirty years passed before the Freedom of Information Act, broadened by Congress in response to the Watergate scandal, forced the FBI to open some of its files on the case. It was only then that the suspicious origin of the atom bomb scene in the Rosenberg apartment first was exposed to public view. The FBI documents divulged that David and Ruth's courtroom stories about their visit to the Rosenberg apartment had no counterpart in any of their signed confessions nor in the transcripts of their rehearsal interviews prior to testifying before the grand jury.

In her July 17, 1950, confession, Ruth Greenglass mentioned nothing about David's September furlough. In his own confession, however, David stated that in September after he arrived in New York

Julius Rosenberg got in touch with me and I met him on the street somewhere in the city. At that time I furnished Julius Rosenberg with an unsealed envelope containing the information I had been able to gather concerning the atomic bomb, as well as a couple of sketches of the molds which make up the atom bomb.

David then provided a description of the atom bomb and added:

I do not know whether Rosenberg read the above information or what disposition he made of it. He did not give me any money for the info at that time.

This statement by David, which said nothing regarding the visit to the Rosenberg apartment about which he would later testify, was not the exclusive possession of the FBI. It was communicated immediately in a memo from J. Edgar Hoover to Attorney General J. Howard McGrath and also to the head of the Justice Department's Criminal Division. Many people were complicit in what was to follow.

I have often pondered the question of why David Greenglass provided his description of the atom bomb to his FBI interrogators. Hard as it is to fathom, his action was entirely gratuitous. David's version of the bomb had no doubt been memorized by him years before from bits and pieces of information he picked up while he was stationed at Los Alamos. I can only suppose that his ability to recite it for the FBI was a source of pride. Vanity was the spur. Like a child performing some special accomplishment for visitors, David was showing off.

Several weeks later, when Ruth was run through her story to ready her for testimony before a grand jury, she still said nothing about the September furlough. She literally made no reference to her return to New York in September, and we now know that the same was true in her actual grand jury appearance. In addition, when Ruth Greenglass was completing her grand jury testimony about Harry Gold's June 1945 visit to their Albuquerque apartment, Assistant U.S. Attorney Myles J. Lane asked her: "Now did David subsequently send any other information to Gold or to Rosenberg?" She replied: "No, he did not."

In David's interrogation prior to his grand jury appearance, he repeated that in September he had met with and given information to Julius, but did not "remember the exact time and place." Prosecutor Lane pressed him for details:

> Q. Was Ethel present on any of these occasions?
> A. Never.
> Q. Did Ethel talk to you about it?
> A. Never spoke about it to me and that's a fact. Aside from trying to protect my sister believe me that's a fact.

When did David and Ruth discard their original accounts, substituting for them the versions they later related in court? Like other researchers, Miriam and I were shocked to learn from the Freedom of Information files that the first reference to the atom bomb scene at the Rosenberg apartment is in an FBI report dated a mere week and a half before the trial. The report simply paraphrases an interview with Ruth; the actual verbatim interview, if it existed, was not released. Another FBI report showed that two days afterward David had been briefed on his wife's latest creation and readily embraced it. These reports were a stunning find. One of the dirty little secrets that had been hidden by the prosecution, the FBI, and the Department of Justice was now exposed. Ever since, the story of the September rendezvous in the Rosenberg apartment, particularly the testimony about Ethel's typing, has troubled students of the case.

In 1979, Sol Stern and Ronald Radosh, preparing an article on the case for *The New Republic*, interviewed David and

Ruth Greenglass with a tape recorder for about an hour. In their article, the writers revealed that the Greenglasses' replies were "so filled with contradiction, lapses of memory and apparent evasions that we went away unconvinced that the typing incident ever took place." Later, when Radosh had co-authored *The Rosenberg File*, he promised during a public meeting at Columbia University to make the Greenglass interview available, but he never did. So I was unable to hear the interview until a few years ago, when one of my journalistic contacts got hold of and passed me a copy of the tape. On it I listened to Sol Stern trying over and over again to elicit from David and Ruth some rational explanation for the lateness of their September stories, but to no avail. It was puzzling. To my mind, their replies made no sense. Furthermore, I was struck by the inability of either of the Greenglasses to give a coherent account of what happened that fateful September day. The whole episode that had sent Ethel to her death in the electric chair seemed to have slipped from their memories. I say "seemed" because I found it impossible to credit that. Something was very wrong with this story.

Next to try was Sam Roberts, author of *The Brother*, who conducted lengthy interviews with David Greenglass. Roberts obtained from David the admission that at the time of the trial he didn't really remember the typing incident he had testified to and had simply followed Ruth's lead. According to Roberts, David told him that "he never remembered Ethel typing his notes. He didn't remember it then, and he doesn't remember it now.'"

After the publication of Roberts' book, CBS News correspondent Bob Simon interviewed David for *60 Minutes II.* In the TV interview, David said, "I don't know who typed it, frankly, and to this day I can't remember that the typing took place. I had no memory of that at all, none whatsoever." David then offered a remarkably muddled version of the September events:

Julius and Ethel were there, and I think my wife was there, and myself. And he asked me to write up some stuff, which I did, and then he had it typed. And I don't know who typed it, frankly. And to this day, I can't even remember that the typing took place, see. But somebody typed it. Now I'm not sure who it was. And I don't even think it was done while we were there.

Greenglass told Bob Simon that Roy Cohn had encouraged him to testify that he had seen Ethel type up the notes. "[Cohn] talked to me and said 'Are you sure?' He says 'Your wife says that your sister typed it,' and I said, 'If she says so.'"

The focus of all these interviews had been on Ethel's typing. Had she typed or hadn't she typed? But the KGB messages that in February 1945 ordered the end of Julius's service as a group leader posed a far larger question. Could Julius, let alone Ethel, have participated in the September events, when he had been dismissed as an agent seven months earlier on direct command from the KGB center in Moscow? Not just the tale about Ethel's typing, but the entire Greenglass testimony about the passage of the atom bomb description in the Rosenberg apartment in September 1945, rested on shaky ground.

There were, however, two solid facts in all this: The Greenglasses *were* in New York City in September 1945. And, as it turns out, there *was* a spy meeting. For the latter information we may again thank Vassiliev, who uncovered yet another critical KGB document. As recounted in *The Haunted Wood*, that document describes a September meeting wholly different from the one testified to by the Greenglasses. It did not take place in the Rosenberg apartment. Neither Julius nor Ethel was a participant. The dramatis personae were David Greenglass and the Soviet agent Anatoli Yakovlev/Yatskov, the man who headed up the KGB's atomic espionage operation in New York. After this hitherto–unknown September meeting with David, Yatskov recounted what had occurred in a cable to Moscow:

> The meeting was quite short, since [Greenglass] had to remain at home that afternoon (it was on the eve of his departure) and broke out [to meet only] for a short while. In our conversation, it was established that [Greenglass] worked in secondary workshops . . . [at Los Alamos], producing tools, instruments for [Los Alamos] and sometimes details for the balloon [the atomic bomb]. Thus, for example, detonators for the fuse of the balloon's explosive were made in their workshop, and [Greenglass] passed to us a cartridge for such a detonator. [He] doesn't have access to the balloon itself or the main shops. Information about

the balloon he is giving us comes from friends who work in [Los Alamos]. . . .

Yatskov then reported that he gave David instructions for the next meeting:

[Greenglass] was assigned to gather detailed characteristics on people he considered suitable for drawing into our work.

In addition [he was given] the task of gathering samples of materials used in the balloon, such as tube alloy [uranium], explosives, etc. Materials sometimes come to [Greenglass's] workshop.[18]

As for Ruth, she was assigned by Yatskov to collect this material from David and pass it to a courier in Albuquerque. The date set for Ruth's meeting? December 21, 1945. This scenario would perfectly explain why the memo conveying David's data to Lavrenty Beria bore the "mysterious date" December 27, 1945.

The documents that support this narrative were uncovered by a group of talented investigators, all of whom, paradoxically, were unaware of the significance of their findings. Working independently with material from two different Soviet archives, two separate teams of researchers—unbeknownst to themselves—had each come up with a part of the story. One part was found by Vassiliev in the KGB files; the other, in the extraordinary Russian Ministry of Atomic Energy archive that preserves real espionage material on the atomic bomb acquired by KGB intelligence agents.

To recapitulate: Yatskov met with David Greenglass in New York City in September 1945. David informed Yatskov that "detonators for the fuse of the [atom bomb's] explosive" were made in the Los Alamos shop where he worked. At an unspecified date, David provided "a cartridge for such a detonator." Yatskov set December 21, 1945, as the date for the next Greenglass meeting and assigned Ruth to collect from David whatever material he wanted to pass on to the Russians.

A meeting presumably did take place on December 21. We know this because a memo was written in Moscow on December 27, 1945, which listed the items received from New York and transmitted to Beria: "materials in English on the construction of an atom bomb" and a sample of "an electrodetonator of the bomb." A second document written in Moscow summarized the transmitted spy report. Labeled "Notes on the Construction of an Atom Bomb, Description of the Construction of an Implosion Bomb," it contains David's signature error, a reference to thirty-six lenses, as opposed to the correct figure of thirty-two. All of these lenses are said to be "five-sided," another error that can be traced directly to David.

Thus, it appears that on December 21, 1945, Ruth Greenglass, having collected from her husband a description of an implosion bomb—destined to become the stuff of history—along with a detonator cartridge that he had stolen and sneaked past the Los Alamos guards, delivered these to the KGB. But we do not know the details. Perhaps a Soviet agent came to Albuquerque to meet with her; perhaps she rendezvoused with someone in another city. However she accomplished her mission, it was not an episode that makes the Greenglasses look like reluctant pawns of the Rosenbergs.

• • •

In the early postwar period, the KGB—unsettled by the defections of Igor Gouzenko and Elizabeth Bentley—suspended their intelligence operations in the United States for about two years. When Russian agents resumed their activities in 1948, they learned that when David Greenglass was discharged from the Army in March 1946, he did not leave empty-handed. Apparently following Yatskov's assignment to him to gather "samples of materials used in the [atom bomb]," he had filched from Los Alamos a chunk of uranium-238 and a sliver of plutonium, the latter in a lead box. Later, David threw the plutonium into the East River; however, he turned the uranium over to the KGB, which sent it on to Moscow.

He also provided the KGB with the names of four espionage prospects, men he had been acquainted with at Los Alamos and who now were at the University of Chicago. The KGB immediately assigned each of them a code name and offered David financial assistance if he would attend the school, but he later reported that he had been unable to gain admission.

David's postwar cooperation with Soviet intelligence continued almost up to the time of his arrest. For example, after David obtained a job with Arma Company, a Brooklyn firm that manufactured stabilizers for tank guns, he offered to take a camera into the plant to photograph drawings of the device. A KGB cable from New York to Moscow on January 13, 1950, described David's secret work at Arma:

> The idea of this device is that it must keep the gun constantly directed at the target regardless of the tank's vibrations while moving during battle.

The New York station reported that it had rejected David's picture-taking as too risky. Instead, David had been asked to make sketches from memory.

It is interesting to observe how David afterward altered this incident into one that exculpated himself and scapegoated Julius. Several months following the executions, he was questioned by Roy Cohn, who by then was chief counsel for Senator Joseph McCarthy's investigating subcommittee. In an affidavit, David stated:

> When I was with the Arma Company during 1949 and 1950, working in their research and development department on various fire control gyroscopic and radar apparatus, Julius asked me to obtain information on the projects upon which I was working. I refused.

David Greenglass's biographer, Sam Roberts, described him as a man who, once he "started talking . . . couldn't stop," an appraisal with which I agree—with one important caveat. Though David was a braggart and a blowhard, he also had a strain of shrewdness and street smarts that enabled him to sometimes put a tight rein on his tongue. He never told the FBI about his September 1945 meeting with Yatskov; about Ruth's assignment to meet a Soviet agent in December; about his thefts of a detonator cartridge, an electric detonator, uranium, and plutonium; or about the information he gave the KGB on the tank gun stabilizer at Arma. And no doubt about much else.

But what he did tell gave the government ample opportunity to be aware that he was a man who could play fast and loose with the truth. He claimed to the FBI that he had been selected to go to an island in the Pacific to help put together one of the atomic bombs later dropped on Japan, but that, because his group leader "knew that Ruth Greenglass was recovering from the effects of a miscarriage, he would not approve the selection of Greenglass." However, when the FBI queried Greenglass's former group leader at Los Alamos, the latter could not confirm any aspect of the story and said that "no member of his group had been even considered" for such a project. He added that Greenglass had "no special ability." So the FBI and prosecution were not uninformed about the proclivities of their star witness.

Ruth had first adamantly denied to the FBI any knowledge of spying about the atom bomb project, then when she came to realize the hole her garrulous husband had dug for them, she threw in her lot with the prosecution. Early on, she devised their survival strategy: She and David were two innocents who had been putty in the hands of the manipulating Rosenbergs. She herself was tough, relentless, and pitiless, especially towards her sister-in-law. The best that can be said for her is that her own predicament was dreadful: She was the mother of two small children, the youngest a newborn infant. Moreover, several months before David's arrest, while pregnant, she had suffered near-fatal burns when her nightgown caught fire from a gas heater in the bedroom of their cold-water Lower East Side flat, after which she had spent nearly ten weeks in the hospital. It was enough to make anyone bitter, and Ruth, who was in her mid-twenties but looked older, was an angry, embittered woman. Her sweet dreams of a "socialist world" of abundance where money would not be needed and "necessities and luxuries" would be available for all were long behind her.

Fortunately for the Greenglasses, their strategy of portraying themselves as easy marks for the designing Rosenbergs in the atomic espionage drama also satisfied the needs of the prosecution. The intent of the latter was to convict both Rosenbergs, by any means necessary, and obtain severe sentences in the hope that the threat to Ethel would cause Julius to break. Though Ruth was never indicted, the possibility that she might be, in a capital case, hung over her as a terrifying menace; meanwhile, David was imprisoned, anxiously contemplating his sentence. In this pre-trial period, the unspoken rules of the game were that the Greenglasses could fashion whatever incriminating scenarios they chose. No documentary evidence or corroborating witnesses to back up their assertions were required. No one on the government side ever questioned any accusatory statement by David or Ruth, no matter to what degree it conflicted with their earlier statements, just so long as it helped to build the atom spy case against the Rosenbergs. Building that case was a joint venture of the prosecution and the Greenglasses.

• • •

After he received his pink slip from Moscow in February 1945, Julius Rosenberg's glory days during World War II as a successful group leader acquiring military-industrial data for Soviet intelligence never returned. But Julius, who had no wish to come in from the cold, took his forced retirement hard and may even have resisted it. His devotion to the Soviet Union and the cause of communism never wavered.

It would be interesting to have a clearer picture of what Julius was up to in the postwar years but, unfortunately, a scarcity of hard evidence makes it impossible to connect all the dots. According to Vassiliev and Weinstein, in May 1948, following the long interruption in Soviet intelligence operations in the United States, a KGB agent renewed contact with Julius. The agent's report gave the New York station operatives cause to feel anxious about Rosenberg's safety. The Moscow center was informed that in 1946–47 Julius had "continued fulfilling the duties of a group handler, maintaining contact with comrades, rendering them moral and material help while gathering valuable scientific and technical information."[19] As to the disposition of this information, the message apparently was silent. Morton Sobell, in a late-life confession made to Miriam and me in 2008, remembered participating in two espionage escapades in the postwar years, both in the summer of 1948.

In December 1948, KGB headquarters in Moscow, worried that the FBI might be bugging its agents, sternly admonished the New York station about Julius's conduct:

> We have special concern provoked by the fact that possibly [Rosenberg] is still engaged in conversations with [agent sources] on the issues of our work at his apartment. . . . It is necessary once more to warn [Rosenberg] categorically about the inadmissibility of such conversations at his apartment or at some of the [agent sources' apartments].

The problem the KGB was having with Julius, as reflected by these 1948 messages, was, I believe, at least partly a generic one that they had often encountered with other Americans with whom they dealt. In the eyes of the exasperated Soviets, many of their American agents were freewheeling individualists who resisted the rules of *konspiratsia*, the rigid code of conduct the KGB tried, often in vain, to instill in them. An essential of this code was to avoid mixing business with pleasure. Agents should not be friends who saw one another socially—let alone lovers or partners in commercial enterprises, as some were. But *konspiratsia* was not compatible with the outgoing American temperament. It was never fully embraced by Julius, nor by others who had been recruited by that supreme maverick of KGB intelligence, the Americanized Jacob Golos.

Even during the active phase of his connection with the KGB, between 1942 and early 1945, Julius fraternized with his sources, and he continued to do so after he was removed from his KGB duties. Max Elitcher, a CCNY college classmate who was the object of a recruitment effort by Julius, testified at the perjury trial of another friend of Rosenberg's, William Perl, about an evening he and his wife had spent in summer 1944 with Rosenberg, Joel Barr, Perl, and others. Questioned by an assistant U.S. attorney, Elitcher recalled that after eating at a Manhattan restaurant the group had gone to Barr's apartment.

> Q. What did you do after you got up there?
> A. . . . We played music. There was a little dancing and we had sandwiches later on. . . .
> Q. Do you recall any of the subjects that were discussed that evening?
> A. Well other than general conversation we talked about a course in music that Joel Barr was taking, and we talked about a music book that he had been using in the course.

Barr then invited everyone to visit a friend of his, Alfred Sarant, who lived in Greenwich Village.

> Q. What did you do after you got there?
> A. Actually, we awakened Sarant, and we were introduced to him. We talked. . . . We played classical guitar music, and he also had some recordings of guitar music which he played for us.

About Christmas 1946, Elitcher testified, he and his wife had dined at a restaurant with Rosenberg, Barr, Perl, and the Sobells. Afterward, everyone had gone to the Rosenbergs' home, where Ethel had prepared a party. Elitcher remembered seeing a Christmas tree and a Chanukah menorah at the apartment. Asked by the prosecutor whether he recalled any of the subjects that were discussed that night, Elitcher replied:

> Well, it was Christmas time, and we talked about the religious upbringing of children, specifically Jewish and Christian children, the problems that are involved in bringing them up.

Needless to say, this sort of lighthearted camaraderie made a travesty of the KGB's *konspiratsia*. But the KGB aside, such rash behavior defied common sense. Ironically, it was one of the reasons that Miriam and I had doubted the existence of the spy ring. The people from whom Julius had obtained information were not just anonymous sources. He had intimate ties with his agents. In his zeal to help the Russians, he had recruited high school and college classmates, longtime friends, and political comrades.

• • •

By 1948, when Julius was contacted again by the KGB, he had reached a personal milestone: He was thirty years old, perhaps a bit over the hill for a young revolutionary. A year earlier, Ethel had given birth to their second son, Robert, and they were still residing in the same cramped three-room apartment. Julius was barely eking out a living operating a small machine shop, and his prospects for the future were bleak. How bleak, he could scarcely have imagined in his wildest nightmares. Within a few years he and Ethel were incarcerated in the Sing Sing death house, controversy about their plight was raging throughout the world, and the American government's message to them was: Confess or die.

But what if Julius and Ethel *had* confessed? Could they have escaped execution if they had tried to meet the government halfway? Perhaps such hypothetical questions are best left to the novelists and playwrights. My own conclusion is that it would have been difficult, probably impossible, for them to save themselves. The only sure-fire way would have been for both, Ethel as well as Julius, to have agreed to everything, including all the atomic espionage deeds they had never done. And then for Julius to have testified at trials and Congressional hearings against the very friends he himself had recruited. Beyond that, Julius was privy to the dark secret that the American Communist Party under Earl Browder had involved itself in enlisting dozens of members for espionage. Disclosing this would have fueled the hysteria of the times and perhaps resulted in mass pickups and incarceration in concentration camps of tens of thousands of Communists and other leftists under the recently enacted Internal Security Act. The Rosenbergs could never have brought themselves to do that.

But many people insist that there must have been some other approach, some clever tactic that would have led to a commutation, at least for Ethel. Suppose Julius had said, "I am guilty but my wife is innocent, all of the Greenglasses' testimony about me was true, but their testimony against Ethel was false," and then had refused to betray others? I am convinced that it would have cut no ice. The government was hardly about to acknowledge that much of the testimony of its primary witnesses, David and Ruth, was spurious, nor to trade the life of Ethel for a mere declaration of guilt by Julius. The Rosenbergs understood what was demanded of them. They knew that to save themselves they had to bite the whole bullet, to pay for their lives with the currency of the times. And that currency was names. It was not a price they were willing to pay.

The fact is that the Rosenbergs were trapped hopelessly. Not until now has it been possible to comprehend how devilishly intricate the trap they were caught in was. Logically, if not legally, the case against them consisted of two separate conspiracies. Julius was guilty in one conspiracy but only marginally involved in the other, while Ethel was guilty in neither. Julius and his buddies had indeed conspired to feed classified data on such subjects as electronics and aeronautics to the Soviet Union. But the atomic bomb conspiracy was a totally different KGB operation. It was headed by KGB officer Anatoli Yatskov and included Harry Gold, Klaus Fuchs, Theodore Hall, Hall's friend Saville Sax, Lona Cohen, David and Ruth Greenglass, and others, both known and unknown. Julius Rosenberg's active connection with the Greenglasses and the Los Alamos project had lasted only a few months before it was severed by the KGB. In that time, he had proposed to Ruth that she recruit David and had passed to the Soviets some relatively trivial Greenglass data about Los Alamos, including the number of employees and buildings, a handwritten plan of the layout of the place, and some general information about what was being done there. Yet as Julius and Ethel listened in court, they heard incredible testimony concocted by the Greenglasses, with the acquiescence of the prosecution, that falsely accused them of receiving lens mold sketches, participating in the cutting of the notorious Jello box, arranging the Albuquerque meeting between Harry Gold and David and Ruth, and, far and away most damaging, receiving the sketch and typing up the descriptive material on "the atom bomb itself."

It was this perjurious testimony—not the military-industrial spying of which Julius was actually culpable—that constituted the evidence on which the death sentences were based. As Julius and Ethel themselves observed in their petitions for clemency, they "had been charged, in the main, with the theft of atomic-bomb information from the Los Alamos Project."

Faced with such an impossible predicament, the Rosenbergs merely denied everything and stuck with this meager stratagem to the end.

But much more than David and Ruth's and Harry Gold's deceptions condemned Julius and Ethel. The government's rhetorical accusations against them were completely over the top, going far beyond mere prosecutorial hyperbole into the realm of the Big Lie. For me, the government's use of the Big Lie is the worst and scariest aspect of the case. Julius found himself in a position analogous to that of a burglar or bank robber being tried as a mass murderer or war criminal. In his opening to the jury, U.S. Attorney Irving Saypol flatly stated that the Rosenbergs, "through David Greenglass," had stolen the atomic bomb. Again, in his summation, Saypol made the government's position clear when he said: "We know that these conspirators stole the most important scientific secrets ever known to mankind from this country and delivered them to the Soviet Union." And just before the sentencing of the Rosenbergs, Saypol commented that "the secrets" they had secured had been of "immeasurable importance," adding: "these defendants have affected the lives, and perhaps the freedom, of whole generations of mankind." All of this set the stage for Judge Kaufman's notorious sentencing tirade, in which he proclaimed that the Rosenbergs' spying, a "crime worse than murder," had "already caused . . . the Communist aggression in Korea, with the resultant casualties exceeding fifty-thousand and who knows but that millions more of innocent people must pay the price of your treason."

Little wonder that the Rosenbergs considered themselves the victims of a crude political frame-up. Nor that to the last minutes of their lives they insisted on their innocence. Of course they lied and lied when they contended that they knew nothing about espionage. Ethel knew about it and Julius had practiced it. But they were aware that at their trial a monstrous web of lies had been spun about them, so perhaps they regarded their own prevarications as petty by comparison and entirely defensible. In their final weeks, when an emissary for the government visited them at Sing Sing to offer clemency in exchange for confessions, Julius—according to Ethel—exploded:

Just imagine! Even if it were true, and it is not, my wife is awaiting a horrible end for having typed a few notes! A heinous crime, "worse than murder," no doubt, and deserving of the supreme penalty. . . .

It is a melancholy commentary that in the technologically advanced United States of America in the middle decade of the twentieth century, the majority of people apparently accepted the veracity of the Big Lie that Julius and Ethel Rosenberg had stolen "the atom bomb secret." Of course even then there were many, both in and out of government, who knew very well that this was a wild fantasy. One of the handful of publications that knew and spoke out, *Scientific American*, referred to "the relative unimportance of Greenglass's data." The Joint Congressional Committee on Atomic Energy also knew. They issued a report designating Greenglass as the "least effective" of the atomic spies. Another who knew was General Leslie R. Groves, wartime head of the Manhattan Project, who later admitted "that the data that went out in the case of the Rosenbergs was of minor value," though he noted that they "deserved to hang." Unfortunately, one of those who apparently did not know was President Dwight D. Eisenhower, who appears to have been woefully misinformed by his advisors. I still wince from embarrassment and despair when I read his fatuous words in a letter to his son:

To address myself . . . to the Rosenberg case. . . . in this instance it is the woman who is the strong and recalcitrant character, the man is the weak one. She has obviously been the leader in everything they did in the spy ring. . . . if there would be any commuting of the woman's sentence without the man's then from here on the Soviets would simply recruit their spies from among women.

Denying executive clemency, Eisenhower said the Rosenbergs' crime "could very well result in the deaths of many, many thousands of innocent citizens." On the day of the executions, Eisenhower upped the ante, declaring:

. . . by immeasurably increasing the chances of atomic war, the Rosenbergs may have condemned to death tens of millions of innocent people all over the world.

So spoke the nation's leader. Over at the Supreme Court, a talented young law clerk named William H. Rehnquist, destined to one day serve as Chief Justice, wrote a memo about Julius and Ethel, lamenting: "It's too bad that drawing and quartering has been abolished." Drawing and quartering! Rehnquist was referring to one of the most savage and painful methods of execution ever devised. It was a crazed period. Praise be to those who did not join the lynch mobs. If anyone has to apologize, it is not those liberals and lefties, including Miriam and myself, who were mistaken in their insistence on the complete innocence of the accused, but correct in their commonsense response that the case smelled to high heaven. No apologies, no regrets.

• • •

It has been a long time. Many people provided the pieces of documentary evidence. I had the joy and excitement of putting those pieces together. If you have ever instantaneously perceived the answer to questions that have eluded you for a prolonged period, but suddenly seem clear, you know how I felt. A flash of insight is an experience that's hard to describe, a combination of relief and exaltation. For a while I enjoyed the feeling. But gradually the tragic implications of the case took hold of me, muting my pleasure.

Now, what particularly moves and pleases me is that it was Michael Meeropol, the elder son of Julius and Ethel Rosenberg, who alerted me to the critical document in Albright and Kunstel. Thus, Michael—who as an 8-year-old boy visited his parents in the Sing Sing death house and promised, "Daddy, maybe I will study to be a lawyer and help you with your case"—played a vital role in helping to reveal a part of the awful but necessary truth about the injustice that cost his mother and father their lives.**

The Rosenberg trial was, of course, shaped by the climate of the times, a climate of pervasive fear bred by the atomic bomb, the Cold War, and McCarthyism. This was the quintessential case of those anxious years. But there was something else—something new and ominous for American criminal justice—that made its appearance in the Rosenberg case and continues to speak to us with growing relevance. It is the role of secret evidence.

** The Rosenbergs' younger son, Robert Meeropol, did become a lawyer. He now directs the Rosenberg Fund for Children, a foundation he established to assist children whose parents are incarcerated or have suffered some form of injury as a consequence of activities in progressive causes.

Secrets are the stock in trade of intelligence agencies. Transparency is the constitutional ideal of our judicial system, in which truth is addressed in open court through a fair adversarial contest. When secrecy and the judicial system become enmeshed, it spells trouble.

We know now that the Rosenberg case had its origins in secret information decoded from intercepted KGB messages. So hush-hush was the decoding project that few if any people outside of the intelligence community knew about it or had access to the documents. Even within the FBI, only a tiny handful of top-level officials actually saw and read the decrypted messages.

It has been frequently observed that if only the FBI had been wise enough to make the secret evidence public before the executions, the widespread protests would have been quieted. But there is a bit of dark comedy here. For ironically, much of the sequestered Venona material relevant to the Rosenberg case actually was exculpatory. Releasing it would have revealed, for example, that of the three defendants, one, Ethel, was the subject of a decoded message that exonerated her as a Soviet spy, and one, Morton Sobell, was not mentioned at all in the decrypts. That alone would have occasioned banner headlines and demonstrations around the world. As for Julius, the preponderance of the decoded documents that referred to him dealt with military-industrial intelligence, not the atom bomb; the information he was shown to have received from the Greenglasses was shockingly insignificant; and none of the decrypts indicated any connection between him and Harry Gold or the notorious Klaus Fuchs, though extensive testimony about the latter was allowed at the trial.

While only the FBI leadership was privy to the contents of the secret evidence, the agents in the field assigned to the case were not ignorant of Venona. True, they lacked the details available to their superiors. And the devil was in the details. But they were the recipients of frequent urgent communications from their Washington headquarters, often signed by Hoover, that contained fragments of decrypted messages. They understood that amazing and vital secret evidence already was in the hands of their bosses. These were the men who conducted the investigation for the trial, collecting documentary proof and interrogating witnesses.

The Sixth Amendment of the Bill of Rights guarantees that the defendant in a criminal prosecution "shall enjoy the right . . . to be informed of the nature and cause of the accusation; to be confronted with the witnesses." But what if the true accusation and witnesses against a defendant were secret, embodied only in a few scraps of intelligence data? What if only a few high officials of the FBI were permitted to view, to analyze, to interpret, or even to know about this data? Would not those high officials have become, in effect, judge and jury in a ghostly secret trial? And having determined guilt to their own satisfaction, would not word of their certainty have reached the ear and affected the conduct of the agent in the field—already pressured with messages such as "I cannot impress upon you too strongly the importance of this investigation"? Would not rumors of secret evidence have been passed about in the councils of state, justifying death sentences to force confessions?

On June 2, 1953, James V. Bennett, director of the Federal Bureau of Prisons, arrived at Sing Sing and met privately with

Julius and Ethel, informing each of them that he had been sent to see them by Attorney General Herbert Brownell, Jr. Afterward Ethel reported to her lawyer that when she told Bennett she was innocent, he responded: "Well, the government claims to have in its possession documents and statements that would dispute that." Ethel said she replied: "If you are persuading me to confess to activities concerning which I have solemnly sworn I have no knowledge, on the basis of evidence with which I was never confronted in court, then obviously the validity of this evidence must be strongly questioned, if it in fact exists at all." She was right, of course. The secret evidence against her, alluded to by Bennett, did not exist at all.

As the time for the executions approached, the FBI was avid for confessions and anxious to forestall any possibility of last-minute executive clemency for the defendants. On June 5, J. Edgar Hoover dispatched a memorandum stamped TOP SE-CRET to Brownell, laying out the case against the Rosenbergs and including, presumably for the first time, some specifics about the secret evidence. Though theoretically Brownell was Hoover's boss, the FBI chief was niggardly in what he was prepared to disclose. He told the attorney general of the United States only that the information came from "a confidential source of unimpeachable reliability whose identity cannot be revealed under any circumstances." When this memorandum was made public decades later under the Freedom of Information Act, the portion of it that apparently describes the secret evidence turned out to be a mere page and a half, and every word had been blacked out. To this day the excised page and a half remains censored, despite years of formal requests by me in an effort to gain its release. So we still do not know what selected tidbits from Venona Hoover chose to share with the attorney general and what he decided to withhold. But Hoover was in the catbird seat; he could reveal or hide bits of his secret evidence as he chose.

At a Cabinet meeting in the White House on the day of the executions, Brownell reportedly told the president and others present that there was "evidence that wasn't usable in court" that corroborated the guilt of the Rosenbergs. Similar assurance was confided to Judge Kaufman immediately after the executions by two FBI agents, who were assigned this curious task by Hoover.

Gradually, in certain elite circles, word spread about the existence of secret evidence. The Nobel Prize–winning scientist Harold Urey, who supported clemency, disclosed this in a speech in 1954.

> I also wish to make a statement in regard to a remark that has come to me from a number of scientists. They say essentially, "Well, if you only knew what I know," or rather mostly, "If you only knew what someone I know knows about the case!" The inference always is that much secret information exists that proves everything but for security reasons, it cannot be made public. My answer is that I do not believe . . . people should be executed on secret evidence.

Two decades later, Miriam and I had our own encounter with "secret evidence" while working as consultants on the public broadcasting TV documentary "The Unquiet Death of Julius and Ethel Rosenberg." One of the researchers on the project interviewed a retired FBI agent, Richard Brennan, who had played a prominent role in the case. Referring to the fact that Harry Gold had originally recalled the password as "Benny sent me" and only much later, under questionable circumstances, had changed "Benny" to "Julius," she asked Brennan about it. He responded with a dismissive gesture. The researcher pressed him: But how then could he be so certain of Julius and Ethel's guilt? Brennan replied with a smile that he knew without any doubt that they were guilty but he could not divulge how he knew. He teased the researcher to try to guess. Of course she could not, but her account to us of his absolute certitude stuck in my mind.

While outside the intelligence community the existence of Venona was a tightly guarded secret, it appears that the FBI concocted a cover story to account for the existence of secret evidence and leaked this phony story to Roy Cohn and perhaps other members of the prosecution team. Harvard law professor Alan Dershowitz recently made public a conversation with Cohn:

> Roy Cohn . . . proudly told me shortly before his death [in 1986] that the government had "manufactured" evidence against the Rosenbergs, because they knew Julius was the head of a spy ring. They had learned this from bugging a foreign embassy, but they could not disclose any information learned from the bug, so they made up some evidence in order to prove what

they already knew. In the process, they also made up evidence against Ethel Rosenberg.[20]

How can an investigation of a case have any semblance of fairness or be conducted within the bounds of due process when those charged with the investigation are convinced that they already know the truth beyond any possibility of doubt? The problems posed for law and justice are not small. For secret evidence is a faceless accuser. It is unimpeachable. Its validity cannot be disputed, its contents scrutinized, its allegations subjected to cross-examination. It exempts itself from public criticism and perhaps from ridicule. It arrogantly demands belief, but evades the responsibility of proof. It makes a mockery of trials.

AFTERWORD

Miriam Schneir

As fate would have it, just a few weeks after Walter's death, a rich lode of new material on the Rosenberg case became available. In May 2009, the "summaries" and "verbatim transcriptions" of documents from the KGB files that Alexander Vassiliev had copied out some fifteen years earlier were at long last opened to public view. Vassiliev donated his original notebooks to the Library of Congress, and the contents were placed online in Russian and in a new English translation by the Cold War International History Project of the Woodrow Wilson Center.

Vassiliev's notes are voluminous, comprising over eleven-hundred pages in eight color-coded notebooks. However, they by no means constitute a vein of pure research gold. For as a former KGB agent, Vassiliev himself cannot be considered an entirely disinterested researcher. In addition, he was not given direct access to the vast KGB archive. Instead, officials of the Russian Foreign Intelligence Service somewhat grudgingly parceled out material to him and did not permit him to photocopy any of it. What his notebooks contain, therefore, is a sampling of KGB documents that were selected by the Russians and that Vassiliev then transcribed by hand—sometimes in full but more often in part, sometimes verbatim but more often in summary form. There is no way to check for possible misinterpretations, omissions, distortions, or slips of the pen, for the originals are at present inaccessible. Yet despite these serious shortcomings, Vassiliev's notes are invaluable, since they are almost certainly as close a look inside the KGB's secret files as we are likely to be permitted for some time.

Students of the Rosenberg case now have available three separate collections purporting to represent what lies within the sacrosanct precincts of the Kremlin archive: the Venona decryptions released in 1995, the KGB cables published in *The Haunted Wood* in 1999, and the Vassiliev notebooks. Each set of documents contains some of the same messages and some that appear nowhere else, and to further complicate matters, each was converted into English by a different translator.

Walter would have been tremendously interested in and excited by the new research treasure trove, but now the task of studying it fell to me. I put aside my own long-term project and set to work reading the notebooks online. As I perused the documents, I searched particularly for any that shed additional light on Walter's four key points: First, that Ethel Rosenberg was not a Soviet spy; second, that Julius did not receive lens mold sketches from David in January 1945; third, that Julius did not cut the Jello box; and finally, that if anyone was guilty of stealing the "secret" of the atomic bomb, it was the Greenglasses, not the Rosenbergs.

• • •

The trial evidence against Ethel was so weak that it seems incredible today that she was even indicted, much less convicted and executed. The only proof of her guilt offered by the prosecution was the Greenglasses' uncorroborated testimony that she helped to recruit Ruth and that she typed David's spy data. When the Venona decrypts were released in 1995, supporters of the government's case highlighted three words in one cable that appeared to confirm Ethel's part in Ruth's recruitment: "LIBERAL [Julius] *and his wife* recommend her as an intelligent and clever girl." (Emphasis added.) Citing this Venona message, the authors of a book published in 2000 chastised Walter and me for continuing to maintain that Ethel was not a Soviet spy. "What the Schneirs ignored," they wrote, "was that both Julius and Ethel had recommended Ruth Greenglass as an agent."[21]

However, even that slim reed can no longer be regarded as corroboration of the Greenglass testimony. As Walter recognized, Julius was not recommending Ruth as an espionage courier but as a person whose apartment could be used as a safe house. Additionally, one of the KGB documents released in 2009 describes the recruitment episode without the damning words "and his wife." It says only, "'Liberal' has recommended Ruth Greenglass" [White Notebook #1, p. 108, file 40129, v. 3a, p. 168].

Allen Weinstein, who for years had exclusive access to Vassiliev's material, dealt with the discrepancy by quoting only the Venona decrypt. Although he cited Vassiliev's White Notebook in his source notes, he did not mention that the cable as it appears there does not contain the crucial reference to Ethel. The authors of *Spies: The Rise and Fall of the KGB in America*,[22] a book added to the espionage bookcase in 2009, cope with the disparity more creatively. They speculate that there were two separate messages, both sent from New York to the KGB center in Moscow, both detailing the same incident, but composed on different dates: the Vassiliev message, on September 20, 1944, and the Venona message, on September 21. *Spies* confidently asserts that a KGB operative in New York informed his bosses in Moscow on September 20 that Julius had recommended Ruth, then sent a "follow-up cable" the next day to notify Moscow of the earthshaking news that "Ethel Rosenberg also vouched for Ruth's reliability."

But the assumption that there were two separate cables— one dated September 20 and another dated September 21— does not take account of the fact that the Venona decryption of this document actually bears two dates, one in the heading, another at the end. As National Security Agency historian Dr. David Hatch explained to me, the date on the bottom indicates when the cable was composed, while the one on top is the date on which it was transmitted. The Venona message in question is dated on the bottom "September 20," which corresponds to the date of the cable in Vassiliev's notebook. (See pages 170–173, for English translations of the Venona cable and the corresponding Vassiliev document.) Thus, although we cannot tell which of the currently available messages is closer to the original, the two-message theory advanced in *Spies* does not hold up.

As for the main charge that sent Ethel to the electric chair—the government's claim that she typed up David's spy data—it still rests entirely on the Greenglasses' uncorroborated testimony. Nothing in the hundreds of thousands of pages released since the trial, including the newly available Vassiliev notebooks, substantiates any aspect of the typing story. Indeed, David himself has repudiated it.

Nor does anything in Vassiliev's notebooks contest Walter's second main conclusion, that "during his January furlough David did not provide the Russians with any lens mold sketches." Revealingly, the book *Spies* also fails to mention any delivery of lens mold sketches to Julius in January. In discussing David's January leave, the authors of *Spies* neatly gloss over the matter of the sketches, remarking only that "Greenglass met with Julius, confirmed his willingness to work for the Soviets, and handed over a description of Los Alamos." The book neglects to point out that if the Greenglasses lied about the delivery of sketches during the January furlough, their testimony that Ethel typed "descriptive material" relating to the nonexistent sketches must have been false as well.

Among the revelations hiding in plain sight that Walter discovered in *The Haunted Wood* was a cable sent by the KGB station in New York to the KGB center in Moscow on February

Reissue (T1362)

From: NEW YORK

To: MOSCOW

No: 1340

21 September 1944

To VIKTOR[i].

Lately the development of new people [D% has been in progress]. LIBERAL[ii] recommended the wife of his wife's brother, Ruth GREENGLASS, with a safe flat in view. She is 21 years old, a TOWNSWOMAN [GOROZhANKA][iii], a GYMNAST [FIZKUL'TURNITSA][iv] since 1942. She lives on STANTON [STANTAUN] Street. LIBERAL and his wife recommend her as an intelligent and clever girl.

[15 groups unrecoverable]

[C% Ruth] learned that her husband[v] was called up by the army but he was not sent to the front. He is a mechanical engineer and is now working at the ENORMOUS [ENORMOZ][vi] plant in SANTA FE, New Mexico.

[45 groups unrecoverable]

detain VOLOK[vii] who is working in a plant on ENORMOUS. He is a FELLOWCOUNTRYMAN [ZEMLYaK][viii]. Yesterday he learned that they had dismissed him from his work. His active work in progressive organizations in the past was the cause of his dismissal.

In the FELLOWCOUNTRYMAN line LIBERAL is in touch with CHESTER[ix]. They meet once a month for the payment of dues. CHESTER is interested in whether we are satisfied with the collaboration and whether there are not any misunderstandings. He does not inquire about specific items of work [KONKRETNAYa RABOTA]. In as much as CHESTER knows about the role of LIBERAL's group we beg consent to ask C. through LIBERAL about leads from among people who are working on ENORMOUS and in other technical fields.

Your no. 4256[a]. On making further enquiries and checking on LARIN[x] we received from the FELLOWCOUNTRYMEN through ĒKhO[xi] a character sketch which says that they do not entirely vouch for him. They base this statement on the fact that in the Federation LARIN does not carry out all the orders received from the leadership. He is stubborn and self-willed. On the strength of this we have decided to refrain from approaching LARIN and intend to find another candidate in FAECT [FAKhIT][xii].

No 751   MAJ[xiii]
    20 September

KGB cable, September 20/21, 1944, from New York to Moscow as decoded and translated by Venona project.

Notes: [a] Not available.
Comments:
    [i] VIKTOR: Lt. Gen. P. M. FITIN.
   [ii] LIBERAL: Julius ROSENBERG.
  [iii] GOROZhANKA: American citizen.
   [iv] FIZKUL'TURNITsA: Probably a Member of the Young
         Communist League.
    [v] i.e. David GREENGLASS.
   [vi] ĒNORMOZ: Atomic Energy Project.
  [vii] VOLOK:
 [viii] ZEMLYaK: Member of the Communist Party.
   [ix] CHESTER: Communist Party name of Bernard SCHUSTER.
    [x] LARIN: Unidentified.
   [xi] ĒKhO: i.e. ECHO, Bernard SCHUSTER.
  [xii] FAKhIT: Federation of Architects, Chemists, Engineers
         and Technicians. See also NEW YORK's message no. 911
         of 27 June 1944.
 [xiii] MAJ: i.e. MAY, Stepan APRESYaN.

28 April 1975

VENONA

White Notebook #1   *108*

p. 168   cipher cable NY to M 20.9.44   Greenglass

> "Liberal" has recommended Ruth Greenglass, his wife's brother's
> wife, for the role of caretaker of the safe-house apartment.
> Young Communist League member since 1942, a typist for the
> electricians' union. According to "L.'s" description, an able
> and smart young woman. Her husband is David Greenglass,
> a mechanic, drafted into the army, is at a factory in Santa Fe.
> Fellowcountryman. "May" requests approval to bring both
> Greenglasses into the fold, with a view to sending her to live with
> David after she is recruited.

Same source   Chester
p. 168   The fellowcountrymen believe that Liberal is connected to
> Chester. Once a month he meets with him to pay membership
> dues. Chester finds out whether we are satisfied with the
> assistance and whether there are any misunderstandings, without
> asking anything about specific work. Since Chester knows the role
> of Liberal's group, May requests permission to obtain leads from
> Chester through Liberal for individuals working on Enormous
> and other types of work.

---

*English translation of KGB cable dated September 20, 1994, as
summarized by Alexander Vassiliev*

17, 1945. This message showed that it was Ruth Greenglass rather than Julius Rosenberg who cut the Jello box recognition device. Another KGB document—now made public for the first time in one of Vassiliev's notebooks—discloses that it was also Ruth who, on her own initiative, set in motion arrangements for the famous June 3, 1945, Albuquerque meeting. The cable that contains this surprising information was sent from New York to Moscow by intelligence agent Anatoli Yatskov in March 1945. Yatskov informed his KGB superiors that a letter written by Ruth shortly after she arrived in Albuquerque "hints that she would like to meet in late May or June." He therefore requested Moscow's permission to send Harry Gold as a courier [White Notebook #1, p. 116, file 40129, v. 3a, p. 380]. Permission evidently was granted, since Gold showed up on the Greenglasses' Albuquerque doorstep on June 3.

Walter's most spectacular argument relates to the cornerstone of the government's case: the September 1945 get-together at the Rosenbergs' apartment during which David allegedly delivered the secret of the A-bomb to Julius. Marshalling evidence from pre-trial FBI statements, grand jury examinations, trial testimony, and a KGB cable made public for the first time in *The Haunted Wood*, Walter demonstrated that the Greenglasses' incriminating account of the September family dinner party was made up out of whole cloth. What really happened in September, Walter suggested, was that David met with the Russian agent Anatoli Yatskov on a New York City street. In a cable describing this sidewalk tête-à-tête to his superiors in Moscow, Yatskov noted that "Caliber" had turned over, at some unspecified time, information on the "balloon" [atomic bomb] and the cartridge for a detonator.

Confronted with Yatskov's report to Moscow—a document that is incompatible with the account the Greenglasses presented at the trial—the authors of *Spies* once again simply folded the contradictory new evidence into the prosecution's Rosenberg-trial script. Thus, they assert that Greenglass "met with Julius on 20 September 1945 and gave him a written description of the bomb that was promptly turned over to Anatoly Yatskov. . . . Yatskov also met briefly with Greenglass on the next day." Yet Yatskov's report makes no reference to any meeting between David and Julius. Nor does it contain any mention of "a written description of the bomb" that Julius purportedly obtained from David and then "promptly" passed along to Yatskov. Even more amazingly, neither the Yatskov cable nor the book *Spies* says a word about Exhibit 8, the all-important sketch that David described as a copy of one he gave to Julius during that September furlough.

The principal source cited in *Spies* for a September meeting between David and Julius is one line in a Vassiliev notebook. That single line consists of a date and a short sentence: "20.09. Caliber handed over materials through Liberal" [Yellow Notebook #1, p. 29, file 82702, v. 1, p. 393]. This sentence appears as the last line on page 29 of Vassiliev's original handwritten notes in Russian. It is disappointing, to say the least, that Vassiliev chose to become so reticent at this critical juncture. Unfortunately, his cryptic entry lacks essential context. It does not tell *where* David passed materials to Julius, *what* the materials consisted of, or *when* they were handed over.

Walter surmised on the basis of the December 27, 1945, transmittal memo brought to light by the authors of *Bombshell* that an espionage meeting at which Ruth Greenglass passed secret information to Lona Cohen probably took place as planned on December 21. The authors of *Spies*, evidently unaware of the significance of the date on the *Bombshell* memo, argued that the meeting never occurred, since KGB activities in the United States were in abeyance at the time. However, Vassiliev's notebooks show that Moscow sometimes rescinded its own suspension orders. For instance, the KGB Moscow center directed the New York station on September 8, 1945 (following the Gouzenko defection in Canada), to immediately suspend Harry Gold's contacts with Fuchs. Then, a few days afterward, Moscow approved a Fuchs-Gold meeting scheduled for later that month.

Pending additional information from the Soviet archives, we cannot be sure whether or not Ruth and Lona kept their December appointment. However, the close coincidence of the two events—the espionage rendezvous scheduled for December 21 and, six days afterward, the memo indicating receipt of Greenglass information in Moscow—is certainly suggestive.

The authors of *Spies* make much of the disclosure in Vassiliev's notebooks that in February 1944, Julius "recruited" another of his personal friends. *Spies* identifies this individual as Russell McNutt, a civil engineer code-named "Persian." But to say that "Persian" was "recruited" by Julius is misleading, for as a Moscow cable later pointed out, "Persian" was "used without his knowledge." After the Russians deactivated Julius in February 1945, "Persian" was put in touch with Anatoli Yatskov, and the two met every two weeks for the next few months. We do not know if the American engineer was aware that Yatskov was a KGB operative.

Spies unequivocally labels "Persian" an "atomic agent." True, Moscow had high hopes for him as a source on "Enormoz," but this expectation was never realized. In his employment at the New York offices of Kellex—a company engaged in the construction of the Oak Ridge, Tennessee, plant for the separation of uranium isotopes—he did not, according to Moscow, "have major opportunities," and he turned down the KGB's urgent appeals that he accept a job at Oak Ridge itself. In May 1945, New York advised Moscow: "In the March-April period, 'Persian' worked on standard computations for water supply and ventilation and did not have any interesting materials at his disposal." In his last meeting with Yatskov he finally provided data of possible value: blueprints and a plan showing the location of equipment in an Oak Ridge building [Yellow Notebook #1, pp. 15, 24, file 82702, v. 1, pp. 225, 310]. "Persian," whose relationship with Yatskov apparently ended at that point, made at most an extremely minor contribution to Soviet atomic intelligence.

• • •

As we researched *Invitation to an Inquest* in the early sixties, Walter and I came to believe that David and Ruth had greatly exaggerated their own and Julius's activities. But now, many decades later, a surprising new narrative of the case has emerged, one that stands on its head what we and millions of others formerly believed. What is finally clear is that the Greenglasses, far from exaggerating their own involvement, actually downplayed it. Contrary to the way they represented themselves at the trial, they were devoted intelligence agents who did as much as they were capable of doing, given David's limited knowledge, to provide atomic information to the Soviet Union. Even the authors of *Spies* acknowledge that David Greenglass's confession was "partial" and that he "held back the full extent" of his espionage. Shrewdly, the Greenglasses offered up the Rosenbergs as stand-ins for themselves.

Julius too was a zealous spy, but he had little to do with atomic espionage. It comes as something of a shock to realize that his active role as the Greenglasses' courier may have lasted less than two months: from early January 1945, when David gave him some general information about Los Alamos, until February, when the Russians suspended him. Through most of 1945, the climactic year in which the first A-bomb was tested and the United States bombed Hiroshima and Nagasaki, Julius's activities were sharply curtailed by the Russians. Even if we assume that he conveyed some indeterminate material from David to a Russian agent in September of that year—an assumption that remains problematic—Julius's overall part in atomic spying was still very slight.

Also striking is how much closer David's pre-trial statements to the FBI were to reality than his accounts to the Rosenberg jury. In his July 17, 1950, confession, for instance, he said nothing about giving lens mold sketches to Julius in January; he described passing information outdoors on a city street in September rather than in the Rosenbergs' apartment; and he never referred to Ethel typing. But by the time of the trial, he had made his bargain with the devil, agreeing to sell his soul in order to save his wife and mitigate his own punishment.

The Greenglass trial testimony was a composite of truths, half-truths, and lies. It was fabricated by Ruth and David in collaboration with unscrupulous prosecutors who were aided and abetted by high-ranking government officials. In saner times, Julius would have received a prison sentence of perhaps fourteen years, the term meted out to Klaus Fuchs in England; and Ethel would have served little or no time. But ambitious and corrupt men held positions of power in the United States. Fear ruled the day, and the will to render reasonable judgments was fatally impaired.

In the aftermath of 9/11, a season of fear settled in once again, bringing with it an erosion of constitutional liberties, infringements of due-process rights, and increased government surveillance. Yet with an administration committed to ending such abuses now in place, the moment may have come for a reconsideration of the trial and executions of Ethel and Julius Rosenberg. To acknowledge the injustices committed in this historic cause célèbre would be a meaningful step toward declaring to the world America's determination to uphold the rule of law.

In his 1978 novel *The Book of Laughter and Forgetting*, Czech author Milan Kundera described the loss of liberties that followed the takeover of his country by a repressive Communist regime. He showed that despite the existence of a constitution that guaranteed freedom of speech, the courts operated as an arm of the government to stifle dissent. Defiantly, Kundera memorialized in his book the names of some of the men and women who were falsely charged with crimes against the state, convicted in sham trials, and hanged. Those in power had hoped by murdering them to erase their names from history; indeed, had hoped to wipe out history itself. But that they could not do. For as Kundera explained, "the struggle of man against power is the struggle of memory against forgetting."

NOTES

1. Arthur Miller, "The Crucible and the Execution, A Memoir," in *Rethinking Marxism: A Journal of Economics, Culture and Society* 2, 3 (Autumn 1989), pp. 68–73.

2. Ronald Radosh and Joyce Milton, *The Rosenberg File: A Search for the Truth* (NY: Holt, Rinehart and Winston, 1983).

3. Robert Louis Benson, *Introductory History of VENONA and Guide to the Translations* (National Security Agency, N.D.), p. 7.

4. *Bombshell: The Secret Story of America's Unknown Atomic Spy Conspiracy* (NY: Times Books, 1997).

5. In 2005, Allen Weinstein became Archivist of the United States after appointment by President George W. Bush and confirmation by the Senate.

6. *The Haunted Wood: Soviet Espionage in America—The Stalin Era* (NY: Random House, 1999).

7. John Earl Hayes and Harvey Klehr, authors with Alexander Vassiliev of the 2009 book *Spies*, claim that Crown publishers, a division of Random House, arranged the project. They assert that Crown "ran into economic difficulties" in spring 1995 and cancelled its contract with the SVR. None of the books was issued by Crown. ["Alexander Vassiliev's Notebooks: Provenance and Documentation . . . ,"] accessed in 2009 at www.wilsoncenter.org/topics/docs/VassilievNotebooks_Web_intro —*M.S.*

8. Some of Walter's questions were answered in 2009 when Vassiliev's original notes were released to the public in their entirety.—*M.S.*

9. The epilogue of the book, pp. 343–44, states without further explanation that "in addition to the material from KGB archives quoted in the preceding pages, the authors collected—but have not cited—150 single-spaced pages of confidential letters, cables, and other documents taken by Moscow's American agents and sources," then adds that some of this material was "actually stolen by British agents— Burgess, Maclean, and Philby."

10. Over three years later, on December 19, 2002, Michael Straight wrote and sent to me some "Notes on *The Haunted Wood*" in which he did remember an encounter in England with the Soviet agent, Arnold Deutsch, whom he had previously said he had never met.

11. The version of this cable made public in 2009 indicates that Moscow was opposed to using Julius Rosenberg as David's contact. It says: "What possibilities are there for approaching 'Wasp,' since it is undesirable for

'Liberal' to participate. After the recruitment 'Wasp' can be turned over to 'Goose' [Gold]" [White Notebook #1, p. 108, file 40129, v. 3a, p. 169].—*M.S.*

12. Vassiliev's notes released in 2009 indicate that he transcribed this document verbatim [Yellow Notebook #1, pp. 54–55, NY to Moscow, Dec. 5, 1944, file 86191, p. 16]. —*M.S.*

13. *The Brother* (NY: Random House, 2001).

14. In 2008, the grand jury testimony of Ruth Greenglass, then deceased, was made public. David refused permission for the release of his testimony.

15. Vassiliev's original notes, released in 2009, indicate that he copied this passage verbatim [Black Notebook, p. 136, June 26, 1945, file 40594, v. 7, p. 131].—*M.S.*

16. The date of this message does not appear in *The Haunted Wood*. Walter obtained it from a reliable source, and I was able to confirm it when Vassiliev's original notebooks were made public in 2009 [Black Notebook, p. 134, file 40594, v. 7, p. 49]. —*M.S.*

17. The release of Ruth Greenglass's and Harry Gold's grand jury testimony disclosed that neither mentioned the Julius password. Ruth testified that Gold identified himself as "Dave from Pittsburgh." Gold testified he spoke a phrase given him by Yatskov, "I bring greetings from Ben in Brooklyn."

18. The original of this cable, as released in 2009, says that David's meeting with Yatskov took place on September 21. "Cartridge" is translated "model," but an endnote explains: "The Russian here, 'patron,' can also be translated 'shell'

or 'cartridge'" [Black Notebook, p. 137, NY to Moscow, Oct. 19, 1945, file 40594, v. 7, pp. 250-51].—*M.S.*

19. This message, as made public in 2009, begins: ". . . despite the fact that his connection with us was interrupted for over 2 years . . ." [Black Notebook, p. 128, file 86192, v.1, p. 173].—*M.S.*

20. *America on Trial* (NY: Warner Books, 2004), p. 323.

21. Herbert Romerstein and Eric Breindel, *The Venona Secrets: Exposing Soviet Espionage and America's Traitors* (Washington, DC: Regnery, 2000), p. 234.

22. John Earl Haynes, Harvey Klehr, and Alexander Vassiliev, *Spies* (New Haven, CT: Yale University Press, 2009). Haynes and Klehr assert in their 2009 introduction to the Vassiliev notebooks (referenced in endnote 7 above) that Weinstein had only "sanitized summaries" of Vassiliev's notes to use. However, several key documents quoted in *The Haunted Wood* are nearly identical to documents in the notebooks, allowing for different translations.—*M.S.*

INDEX

Note: Page numbers in bold refer to illustrations